Don Wulffson

Before Columbus

Early Voyages to the Americas

 Twenty-First Century Books
Minneapolis

For Fletcher
—DLW

My thanks to my wife, Pam, for her tireless research and invaluable support

Text copyright © 2008 by Don Wulffson
Maps by Jeff Del Nero

Twenty-First Century Books
A division of Lerner Publishing Group, Inc.
241 First Avenue North
Minneapolis, MN 55401 U.S.A.

Website address: www.lernerbooks.com

Library of Congress Cataloging-in-Publication Data

Wulffson, Don L.
 Before columbus: Early voyages to the Americas / by Don Wulffson.
     p. cm.
 Includes bibliographical references and index.
 ISBN-13: 978-0-8225-5978-8 (lib. bdg. : alk. paper)
 1. America—Discovery and exploration—Pre-Columbian. 2. America—Antiquities. I. Title.
 E103.W855 2008
 970.01'1—dc22
                                                                                2005024487

Manufactured in the United States of America
1 2 3 4 5 6 – JR – 13 12 11 10 09 08

TABLE OF CONTENTS

INTRODUCTION

For 469 years, virtually everyone who had heard of Columbus's voyages believed that he was the first European to cross the Atlantic to America. Not until 1960, with the unearthing of Leif Ericsson's thousand-year-old settlement in North America, at L'Anse aux Meadows in Newfoundland, was it proved that the Vikings had set foot on the continent long before Columbus.

And now historians and archaeologists are finding indications that the Vikings may have been just one of many ethnic and cultural groups—Chinese, Phoenician, African, Welsh, and Irish among them—to arrive on American shores long before the famous Genoese explorer.

Can any of these early expeditions to American shores be proved beyond doubt? Some can, but most cannot. However, the evidence is abundant and thought-provoking enough that Before Columbus *may change how you see America's ancient past. I can only present the archaeological findings and historical theories— and recount these strange, sometimes brutal but always interesting stories—and allow you to draw your own conclusions.*

—Don Wulffson

A detail of a carved stone head from the Olmec civilization of Mexico (ca. 1000 B.C.–A.D. 1100)

GREENLAND

ICELAND

NORTH AMERICA

EUROPE

480 B.C.

310 B.C.

Carthage

146 B.C.

Corvo

Sidon
Tyre

AFRICA

ATLANTIC OCEAN

SOUTH AMERICA

N

W   E

S

0   400   800 mi

0   400   800 km

CHAPTER 1
FREEDOM OF SACRIFICE

Phoenicians
146 B.C.

The Phoenician civilization began to develop around 3000 B.C. in what today is the country of Lebanon. Because most of their land was unsuited to farming, they became a nation of seafaring traders. By 800 B.C., the Phoenicians had become the most powerful merchants and colonizers in the Mediterranean world—and archaeological evidence indicates that some of those colonies may have been in North and South America.

Instead of a single large piece of land, the Phoenician nation was made up of three narrow, separate coastal areas and several islands and portions of islands. Out of necessity, the Phoenician ships were the finest of their day. Because of their large and powerful fleet and expertise in navigation, the Phoenicians traveled great distances by sea. According to the sixth-century Greek historian Herodotus, the Phoenicians undertook a three-year voyage in which they were able to circumnavigate (sail around) Africa. Equally as impressive, they sailed to Spain, Iceland, Britain, and Scandinavia

Phoenician ships were known for their seaworthiness. This stylized drawing of a bireme (ship with two banks of oars) warship features a removable sailing rig and the typical upward-thrusting stern (rear).

(northern Europe) and established camps and settlements in many of these places. They even sailed to Corvo, one of the two westernmost islands in the Azores (islands in the north Atlantic). Corvo is about 1,200 miles (1,931 kilometers) from the North American mainland.

Though the exact number is not known, the Phoenicians established at least fifty colonies during their travels, several of which may have been in North and South America.

Their defeat and conquest at the hands of the Greeks was the moving force behind the Phoenicians heading toward North and South America. Off and on, from 480 to 146 B.C, the Greeks battled the Phoenicians for control of the Mediterranean, fighting on both land and sea. Ultimately, this incredibly long war—of more than three hundred years—ended in disaster for the Phoenicians. Routed on the battlefield, many of their cities in ruins, they lay down their arms. Humiliated, they watched as the Greeks took their land.

In most ways, the Greeks were neither harsh nor demanding rulers. But there was one thing—a ritual of the Phoenician religion—they would not tolerate. In the ritual, a man, woman, or child was laid on a grooved stone altar and then sacrificed to the gods.

In 1749 a pot full of Phoenician coins was found on Corvo.

Phoenician merchant ships were broad beamed, providing not only large cargo space but also the ability to withstand heavy seas. These ships, known as round boats, relied heavily on sails rather than rowing. The image below is from a relief found in Sidon, Phoenicia's oldest city.

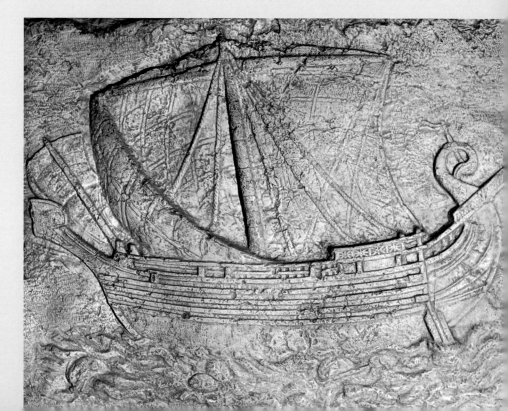

After their defeat, the Phoenicians tried to conduct their bloody rituals in secret. They built stone altars deep in forests and caves, and they continued sacrificing people. Relentlessly, the Greek soldiers tried to eradicate the practice. They sought out those who engaged in the ritual, and those found guilty were imprisoned or enslaved.

Many Phoenicians concluded there was only one choice: to escape. And they would head, it was decided, to western Africa, where they had already explored and established a few settlements on the coast. They would expand these and create a new Phoenicia, a new home where they could live and worship as they pleased.

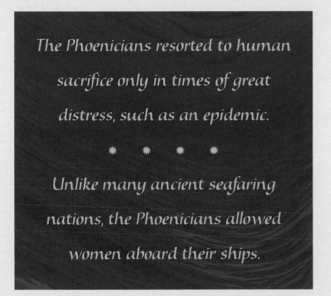

The Phoenicians resorted to human sacrifice only in times of great distress, such as an epidemic.

❉ ❉ ❉ ❉

Unlike many ancient seafaring nations, the Phoenicians allowed women aboard their ships.

Though Phoenicia was a conquered land, many of the merchant ships in the harbors were still operated by Phoenicians. At night, provisions for large numbers of Phoenician men, women, and children were smuggled aboard. When all was ready, the ships slipped away, some on their own and some in convoys, all headed to western Africa.

Not many made it. Some sank in storms, and others were overtaken by Greek warships and destroyed. And several, carried by the powerful force of prevailing winds and currents in these regions, were swept helplessly southwest, in the direction of the Americas.

Recent findings indicate that the Phoenicians may have made two large-scale landings on the eastern coast of the United States. One group reached present-day New Hampshire. The other sailed into what is now Chesapeake Bay.

Those who headed south to the bay made a brief landing to reprovision their ships and then sailed up the Susquehanna River. They followed its winding, 250-mile (402 km) course until waterfalls near the present site of Harrisburg, Pennsylvania, stopped them.

A strange collection of buildings provide possible evidence of the Phoenicians' presence at the New Hampshire site. Known today as America's Stonehenge, the place is unlike anything else in North America. Consisting of more than twenty stone structures, there are enormous stone ramps, walkways, and a system of underground drains to keep the site clear of rainwater.

According to local legend, this curious collection of stone structures was built in colonial times by an eccentric old man named Jonathan Pattee and his five strapping sons. That story unravels rather quickly, however. To begin with, historical documents

No one can actually prove who built what is known as America's Stonehenge in Salem, New Hampshire. A maze of chambers, walls, and ceremonial meeting places, it is most likely the oldest human-made construction in the United States. It is more than four thousand years old.

show that Pattee's only son died in infancy. Instead, he had four daughters. They may have been strong girls, but certainly not strong enough to lift huge stone slabs, some of them weighing upward of 50 tons (45 metric tons).

Amid the various buildings is the strangest—and most important—structure of all: a nearly rectangular sacrificial stone. Slightly wider at the top, the stone is the size of an outstretched human form. It is built on a slant, and a 2-inch-deep (5 centimeter) runoff channel drains from its top to its base.

A second slab for human sacrifice, almost identical to that at America's Stonehenge, has also been discovered. Only 50 miles (80 km) from the first stone, it was found deep in the woods near Leominster, Massachusetts.

Nothing similar to these two large sacrificial slabs has ever been found in New England—or anywhere else in the United States. Neither the Native Americans nor the colonists had use of such items. And

This 4.5-ton (4-metric ton) grooved slab still remains one of the most controversial parts of the America's Stonehenge site. Its overall size, the oracle speaking tube beneath, and the carved channel on the top of the table all indicate that it was intended for sacrifices.

neither indulged in human sacrifice. This leaves the intriguing and plausible scenario of the Phoenicians settling in this area.

The slabs and buildings, however, are not the only evidence. One day in 1948, Philip Beistline, a retired teacher in Mechanicsburg, Pennsylvania, was pursuing his hobby—searching the woods near his home for arrowheads and other Native American artifacts. He happened upon a fist-sized stone that bore extremely unusual markings.

Beistline mailed the stone to Cornell University in New York. The professor who examined it said that he couldn't be sure, but the markings appeared to be Phoenician.

The following year, Dr. William Strong, a man who lived in the same area, also found one of the stones. Then he discovered several others. Fascinated, Strong undertook the hunt for more such stones. For years he scoured the woods, each day finding more and more of them. When finally he'd finished, Strong had collected almost one thousand of the oddly etched rocks!

One of the most puzzling things to Strong was that most of the stones had duplicates. In many cases, dozens of them bore the exact same inscription. Baffled by the things, Strong showed them to all sorts of experts, but they had no idea what the inscriptions meant. Then he showed the curious stones to Dr. George Radan, an expert in Middle Eastern languages. Radan surprised Strong. "It's Phoenician," said Radan. Then he commenced to read it! "Aleph, Beth, Gimel, and Daleth," said Radan. "They're letters of the Phoenician alphabet."

Instead of handwriting, the Phoenicians had arranged the stones to

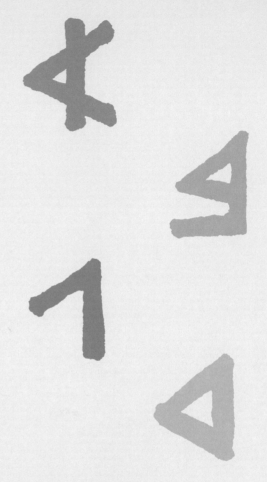

The Phoenician alphabet consisted of relatively simple angular shapes, such as the equivalents of A (aleph), B (beth), C (gimel), and D (daleth), from top above. Could natural causes have etched these crisscrossing lines into the Pennsylvania stones? No one is sure.

spell out words. Also, as was their practice, they had used letters as numbers—and as traders, they would have constantly been using this numbering system. Finally, it is reasonable to assume that the stones served as teaching devices. Just as children today sometimes use lettered blocks to learn the alphabet, the Phoenicians used inscribed stones. It is for these reasons that such a great number of duplicates had been needed.

Some say that Native Americans made the etched stones. But if so, then how did it come about that they were writing in Phoenician? Others say the stones were etched by natural erosion. But this brings up a similar question: why did they erode into letters—Phoenician ones?

> In Texas and New Mexico, inscriptions in stone have been found that are a combination of Hebrew and Phoenician, a style of writing used in Phoenicia as far back as 1000 B.C.

Another find by archaeologists working near the Mechanicsburg site were stacks of flat building stones, about seventy-five in all. Each stone was 30 inches (76 cm) long, 18 inches (46 cm) wide, and had V-shaped grooves cut into the sides exactly 6 inches (15 cm) apart. Clearly, they were building stones. By means of the V-shaped grooves, the stones interlocked so perfectly that no mortar would have been needed to make a tight, permanent connection.

Something else was obvious about these stones. They had never been used. Rather, they gave the appearance of having been carefully made and stacked in readiness to construct a temple or other important building. But construction was never started.

Why? The Phoenicians appear to have vanished quite suddenly, shortly before work was to begin. One possibility is that illness overtook the colony. Another is that they were killed or driven off by Native Americans.

✳ ✳ ✳ ✳

Those Phoenicians aboard the ships that were swept all the way down to South America seem to have also suffered a grim fate.

In 1872 an engineer named Francisco Pinto discovered more than twenty caves in the jungles of Brazil. In all of them were rocks of the kind found in Pennsylvania, with an inscription on each. For months, Pinto labored, collecting almost 250 stones. Years later, in 1911, the Brazilian government invited Dr. L. Schoenhagen, a German linguist, to visit the country to examine the inscriptions. Not only did he verify that the stones bore Phoenician letters, but he became so enthralled with the discovery that he remained in the country for the next fifteen years—writing and lecturing on Phoenician voyages to the region.

There have been numerous other discoveries of Phoenician writing in caves throughout Brazil. Perhaps the most important are those found by Ernest Ronan. In the early 1880s, the French scientist, working with a team of Brazilians, discovered a cave that contained, instead of random stones containing letters of the alphabet, a written message in Phoenician. Translated, it read:

I arrived with my companions and thirty workers in four boats after a long and dangerous journey . . . After walking a few days inland we arrived at this mountain where we found many ores and mines. We worked here for sixteen years and acquired much gold, copper and valuable jewels. (Signed): Eklton, Commander

Seemingly, all was going well at first. But later writings paint a very different picture. Called the Parahyba Inscriptions, they are messages of despair. They tell of unbearable heat, insects, snakes, human-eating animals, hostile local peoples, and disease. They tell of death.

Though the Phoenician settlements in North and South America ended in failure, it can't be said that all the Phoenician colonists and their offspring simply perished and disappeared. Over the years, from the late nineteenth century through the twentieth century, there have been countless sightings of individuals and tribes of light-skinned indigenous peoples—in both North and South America. Some are described as having Semitic—or Phoenician—physical characteristics. It is very possible that some could be descendants of the few survivors of the numerous but unsuccessful efforts by the Phoenicians, so many centuries ago, to establish colonies in the New World.

GREENLAND

ICELAND

NORTH AMERICA

EUROPE

Rome

A.D. 64

ATLANTIC OCEAN

AFRICA

SOUTH AMERICA

N

W   E

S

0   400   800 mi

0   400   800 km

CHAPTER 2
FLIGHT OF THE ROMAN CHRISTIANS

Romans

A.D. 64

In A.D. 64, Roman Christians suffered some of the worst religious persecution in history. In horrid public spectacles, thousands were beheaded, crucified, or eaten by wild animals. Many fled, both by land and sea. Of the latter, there is recent evidence to indicate that some of them may have landed and settled in America—more than fourteen hundred years before Columbus.

The story begins with the death of Jesus Christ and the beginning of a new religion, Christianity, based on Jesus' teachings and recognition of him as the embodiment of God. The religion spread incredibly fast—from Jerusalem, through the Middle East, and up into Rome.

From the outset, the polytheistic (worshippers of many gods) emperors and citizens of Rome took a dislike to the monotheistic (worshippers of one god) Christians. Treated as outcasts, Christians stood aloof from others. Doing so made them seem all the more suspicious.

Still, though they were ridiculed and scorned, their presence was tolerated. This changed dramatically for the worse when Nero became emperor of Rome in A.D. 54.

Only sixteen when he took power, Nero grew to become one of the cruelest and most bizarre emperors in Roman history. He considered himself an actor, poet, and musician, and put on one-man shows that lasted for hours and from which it was forbidden to leave. Those who fell asleep were slapped awake. People began feigning illness—even death—in order to be carried outside.

Nero sang, wrote poetry, and acted. He was—or at least, tried to be—a man of the arts. At the same time, at the Circus Maximus, Rome's spectator venue that held up to 150,000 people, he delighted in bloody spectacles and even thought up some of the most horrid of these displays himself.

Unlike earlier emperors, Nero was not the least bit tolerant of the Christians. The fact is he despised them from the start. Why? In addition to their own deities, people of other religions were expected to worship the Roman gods, such as Mars (the god of war) and Venus (the goddess of beauty).

The Christians refused.

Infuriating Nero even more was that Christians put God before him. Nero believed that *he* was God and should be worshipped above all others.

Again, the Christians refused.

Nero declared that this showed contempt, not only for himself but also for Rome. It revealed, the emperor ranted, that the Christians hated the world, civilization, and even humanity.

Untrue but extremely frightening rumors began circulating around Rome that Christians were cannibals, criminals, and baby killers, who wanted to murder anyone who did not share their beliefs. In his first effort to rid himself of the stubborn Christians and the imagined menace they posed, Nero had Peter, one of Christ's apostles, executed. The Christians' leader was arrested as an atheist, given a mock trial, and immediately sentenced to crucifixion. Dragged before a screaming crowd, he said that he was not worthy of dying in the same way that Jesus had and asked that he be crucified with his head downward. In that position, dying slowly, he gave a sermon to the crowd.

Christians throughout Rome lived in ever-mounting fear. Increasingly, they were mocked and beaten. To protect themselves, they spoke of their religion only behind closed doors. In the streets, they recognized one another by drawing an X, a fish, or another sign in the air or dust. They further showed their belief by carving chrismons—art with symbols and letters combined—on walls, trees, and other places.

The Christians tried hard not to draw Nero's attention or do anything that would give him an excuse to further torment them. It didn't save them. The perverse emperor found an excuse, anyway.

On the night of July 18, A.D. 64, a large fire broke out in Rome. Because of strong winds and because the city at this time was made mostly of wood, the fire quickly got out of control. For six days and seven nights, the fire raged. First, the conflagration roared through the level areas of the city, obliterating them and killing untold thousands in the narrow streets. Then it raced uphill in monstrous flaming arcs, consuming all in its path.

When the fire was finally extinguished, only four of Rome's fourteen districts remained intact. Two-thirds of the city was nothing but blackened rubble.

Nero's behavior was never more bizarre than the evening in A.D. 64 when he played his lute to accompany his songs of joy while the city of Rome burned.

From the outset, many Romans believed that Nero set the fire. The emperor was the prime suspect for several reasons.

Why? Nero had long wanted to rebuild Rome on a grand and imposing scale and rename it Neropolis. Nero's new Rome would be the centerpiece of the world of art, and his own home, the centerpiece of the city, lavish and magnificent beyond compare. He would call it the Golden House.

For Nero's dream to come true, the city would first have to be destroyed. Not only would a huge fire clear the land, so to speak, but it would also create the need for a new city. Nero was already drawing up plans when the fire broke out.

And there was still more incriminating evidence: On the first night of the fire, Nero appeared onstage at a private party. While playing a lyre, a type of harp, he sang of the legendary destruction of ancient Troy. It was certainly not lost on his audience that this bizarre emperor, instead of being at all alarmed, sang of the destruction of one civilization while his own capital was burning.

Then came the most damning evidence of all. During the blaze, many of Nero's servants and "friends," armed with tar and blazing torches, were seen setting fires and forcibly preventing others from trying to extinguish the flames.

With every finger pointing at him, Nero found himself in immediate need of a

While it is known that Nero blamed the fire in Rome on the Christians, it has never been proved that he started it. Some historians say the evidence against him was concocted by his enemies and, in all likelihood, the fire started and spread naturally. Moreover, to Nero's credit, after the fire, he organized relief efforts and opened public buildings, including his own palace, as temporary shelters for the homeless and fed them at his own expense.

Additionally, the government, at his instigation, enacted stricter building codes and improved the city's firefighting facilities.

Nero went beyond the bounds of meting out justice for alleged crimes and made the torture and burning of Christians into a public spectacle.

scapegoat. The Christians. He declared that they had set the fire and must be punished for their terrible crime.

The bloodshed began.

Nero immediately had his soldiers arrest large numbers of Christians. They were thrown into cages and dungeons. Tortured mercilessly, they eventually admitted setting fire to Rome and to every crime of which they'd ever been accused—devil worship, cannibalism, treason, and baby killing. To stop the terrible pain, they confessed to anything and everything and even gave the names of other Christians—other arsonists. Mock trials were held. Hundreds of Christians were sentenced to death.

Some committed suicide, wracked with guilt at having succumbed to torture. The rest were led in chains into the Circus Maximus. Some were beheaded. Others were dressed in reeking, uncured skins of wild animals. As the crowd cheered, lions and packs of starving dogs were let loose in the arena to literally tear them to pieces.

Burning to death was the sentence of some Christians. Drenched in oil and naphtha (a highly flammable substance), they were crucified and then set ablaze. Nero was especially fond of this horrid type of execution. He staged chariot races at night, with illumination provided by the flames.

Most of the Roman people saw through Nero's scheme. Very few were tricked into believing the Christians had started the fire. And though Romans were very accustomed to seeing bloody gladiatorial battles, Nero's perverse, seemingly endless butchery of the Christians was more than even they could bear. The killings had become nauseating. Instead of turning the people against the Christians, as Nero had hoped, the persecutions created sympathy for them.

People hid Christians in their homes. In horse-drawn carts and on foot, Christians were smuggled to safety. Some fled by sea.

Roman ships of the time were powerfully built, and they were of two types: cargo ships and warships. The cargo ships were huge sailing vessels that could carry as much as 1,000 tons (900 metric tons) of cargo and as many as a hundred passengers. For the most part, it was in these cargo vessels that the Christians fled. Their flight by sea (and other means) is well known. But exactly how many attempted to escape in this manner—and in how many ships—are details unrecorded by history.

Roman warships attacked many of these fleeing vessels. Archers rained arrows on the Christians. Catapults unleashed huge stones and incendiary bombs. And massive iron rams tore into the vessels, splintering beams and tearing gaping holes in their sides. Those who survived the impact and the ship's sinking were left to drown.

At that time, the Roman Empire included most of Europe, North Africa, and Britain. The only direction in which the Christians could flee was west, across the Atlantic. Though Earth was then thought to be flat, it was also widely believed that there was a vast, unknown land somewhere to the west, across the Atlantic. Some of the ships may have sought out other destinations. However, the most natural course for them was

that which would take them to present-day America.

Like all freighters of the time, Roman cargo ships were primarily designed for carrying trading goods. Travelers were welcome, but their comfort was given little attention. The ships had a few cabins for important people, but the rest lived on the open decks. They had only tents and small, crude shelters to protect them from the elements. Small iron braziers provided heat and were used to cook food.

The captain of such a vessel had few navigational aids. The steering gear was an oar-shaped rudder on the right rear quarter of the ship. Other equipment consisted only of a device called a sounding line—a weighted cord to determine depth—and heavy iron cups for dredging up samples of the sea bottom. A Roman ship's captain did not even have a compass. By day he had to navigate by landmarks. By night he had only the stars and moon.

What they lacked in navigational instruments, these Roman ships made up for in terms of size, strength, and seaworthiness. As sturdy as they were thick, the hulls were usually covered with sheets of lead below the waterline. They also had a layer of tarred fabric between the wood and lead skin.

Roman cargo ships had a capacity of about 250 tons (227 metric tons). It is estimated that one such as this model represents would have been about 90 feet (27 meters) long.

Compared to Columbus's ships, they were larger, stronger, and more seaworthy. For example, Roman ships were up to 180 feet (55 m) in length. The largest of Columbus's three ships, the *Santa Maria*, was 117 feet (36 m). Crossing the Atlantic was well within the Romans' capabilities.

It is not known how many of these ships survived the crossing. Some were lost to the Roman fleet and some probably to the elements. But there is solid evidence that at least one of the vessels succeeded in reaching North America—the present state of Virginia, to be exact.

In the words of historian Charles Boland, "They came in ships, sailing out through the Pillars of Hercules [natural formations between Spain and Morocco] and across the unknown Atlantic, until they made landfall off . . . Hatteras Island [off the coast of North Carolina]. They coasted several islands, and then found the Roanoke River, and sailed up its winding course until they reached Clarksville, in Virginia. They moored their ship and set out to explore the countryside."

The Christians would have found a beautiful land, one of fertile fields; lush forests; and a wonderful maze of interconnecting rivers, streams, and lakes. Fish and game were plentiful. The weather was moderate. Living in this part of Virginia at the time was a Siouan tribe known as the Occaneechi. Most likely, it would have been amid these people that the Christians lived.

On what evidence do Boland and others base their conclusions about the Roman Christians? How do they know the route taken or the eventual destination? What proof is there that Roman Christians actually settled in Virginia among the Occaneechi?

The story did not begin to emerge until 1943. In that year, a man named James Howe bought a large farm in Virginia alongside the Roanoke River. A retired historian,

Howe planned to spend most of his time writing and relaxing.

One day, while digging in a small vegetable garden, Howe's shovel hit a piece of iron. Examining it, he could see that it was a handmade item and extremely old. Intrigued, he continued digging and found more pieces. Eventually, Howe had 400 pounds (182 kilograms) of iron.

Native Americans hadn't made it, he knew, since no tribes in North America ever worked with that metal. Thus, the iron must have been from colonial times, Howe concluded, and his land was on the site of an old colonial forge.

He very quickly found that this wasn't the case.

The history of the land he had bought was well known. Newspaper and magazine articles, books, pamphlets, and official records all told its story.

The huge estate had belonged to Major John Nelson, a U.S. officer and hero of the American Revolution. The major had received it as a gift in 1782 in appreciation for his service to his country. But neither he nor his heirs ever developed the land. When Howe purchased part of it in 1943, it was still as wild as it had been during the American Revolution.

In Howe's opinion, only one conclusion was left: long before the arrival of the European colonists, people who knew how to smelt iron had lived in the area. The iron had been handmade by a very old, primitive process—one used almost exclusively by the Romans.

Searching for more answers, Howe continued digging. Only 18 inches (45 cm) down, he saw the glint of metal. But it wasn't iron. Digging carefully, with his hands and a small knife, Howe slowly exposed a bronze cup. A jagged piece was missing, but it was otherwise in good condition.

Fascinated by the strange cup, Howe began researching it. First, he had the metal tested. It was bronze—an alloy of copper and tin. And it was from 1 to 2 percent silver—the formula most commonly used by the metalworkers of ancient Rome. Further research showed that it was almost identical to six cups discovered in Pompeii, the Roman city destroyed by the eruption of Mount Vesuvius in A.D. 79.

In a period of a few months, Howe unearthed three more bronze items. Two were just fragments, and it was impossible to tell what they had once been. But the third was something called a spindle whorl, a rounded brass rod of a kind common in ancient Rome.

In 1943, just as Howe was beginning his discoveries, magazines and newspapers had come out with stories about another discovery—one that Howe found very interesting in the light of his own findings. Only 60 miles (97 km) from his farm, a natural draft furnace was unearthed. Its design was that used by Roman blacksmiths for centuries.

Howe turned his full energies to solving the fascinating mystery. More digging and searching turned up numerous artifacts—several small knives, a thrusting sword, chisels for cutting stone or metal, and an ancient device for making nails—one invented by the Romans.

Seven years later, perhaps the most important discovery of all was made. Howe first learned of it in May 1950, in a newspaper article in the *Richmond Times Dispatch*. According to the article, two strangely marked rocks had been found in Virginia, in the vicinity of Howe's farm. Professionals agreed the writing on the rock was very ancient and had been inscribed in an unknown language, but as yet, no one had been able to decipher it. In conclusion, one scholar wrote, "[The writing] on the rocks is very interesting and very important . . . but there is not much possibility of interpreting the signs."

Howe hurried to the location—only 20 miles (32 km) from his home. There, he found two other ironworking sites and then the rocks. After weeks of study, Howe and other experts realized they weren't looking at writing. The marks were **chris**mons.

The chrismons were extremely important. Until they were found, there was no proof that Christian—rather than pagan (polytheistic)—Romans had lived in the area. The ancient symbols were the final piece of the puzzle.

What became of the Roman Christians? In the opinion of Boland and other experts, most likely they melded with the Native Americans. They lived in peace. Unlike later foreign visitors to the native people's homeland, they did not come to **tak**e the land or change it. They came only as refugees needing safe haven. Over time, more than fourteen hundred years, they intermarried. Their blood intermixed, and they were part of the genetic pool when Europeans arrived centuries later.

What became of Nero? The Roman people, the senate, and even his own guards turned their backs on the man. After two failed assassination attempts, he fled to a country villa. Cornered there by his own soldiers, he committed suicide at the age of thirty.

In his short reign of fourteen years, he caused the deaths of thousands and almost destroyed an empire. But he might have been the moving force behind one of the strangest pre-Columbian voyages to America, that of the Roman Christians.

ARCTIC OCEAN

GREENLAND

RUSSIA

ICELAND

Alaska

Canada

NORTH
AMERICA

EUROPE

CHINA

Beijing

A.D. 458

PACIFIC OCEAN

Fusang
(Mexico)

Florida

ATLANTIC

AFRICA

Caribbean Sea

Cape
Verde
Islands

Spice
Islands

A.D. 499

SOUTH
AMERICA

OCEAN

AUSTRALIA

INDIAN

New
Zealand

OCEAN

N

W   E

S

South
Shetland
Islands

0   750   1500 mi

0   750   1500 km

ANTARCTICA

CHAPTER 3
FUSANG: FROM CHINA TO AMERICA

Chinese A.D. 458 and 1421

The Phoenicians and Romans may have sailed to the east coast of the Americas. The Chinese may have sailed to the west coast, arriving about four hundred years after the Romans and more than one thousand years before Columbus.

The amazing story of a Chinese discovery of America begins with the life of a Buddhist monk named Hoei-Shin. In A.D. 458, Hoei-Shin and twelve followers sailed with a convoy across the Pacific to spread the Buddhist faith. Forty years later, he returned with a tale of a 7,500-mile (12,068 km) voyage to a land he called Fusang. There is reason to believe that Fusang was ancient Mexico.

Upon his return in A.D. 499, Hoei-Shin told his story to anyone who would listen. He said that he was one of a few survivors of a convoy to Fusang. Storms, battles, and illness had taken the lives of most of the others.

Because the tale told by Hoei-Shin was so fantastic, some people thought the elderly monk must have made it up. Of the many who believed him was a scholar named Yao Silian. In the early sixth century, Yao wrote

In 1972 the remains of an ancient Chinese shipyard were unearthed on the coast of southern China. The ships being produced in the place were made of wood and iron, and they were extremely large—as large as those described by Hoei-Shin.

a fifty-six-volume work titled *History of the Liang Dynasty.* In it he included the story of Hoei-Shin, sometimes quoting directly from the old man's diary.

Yao said that nine vessels, including one carrying Hoei-Shin, departed China in 458, headed across the "Great Eastern Sea" (the Pacific). During the voyage, they were attacked by pirates, encountered a series of storms, and several ships were lost, both in battle and in the raging tempests.

The voyage took almost "three moons" (months) and was the longest yet undertaken by the Chinese. "Fusang," said Hoei-Shin, was "twenty thousand *li*" from China. This is 7,500 miles (12,068 km), which is extremely close to the actual distance between China and Mexico.

Since the third century, Chinese mariners had an odometer-type device that enabled them to determine the length of voyages. The fact that more than fifteen hundred years ago, they knew the actual distance between China and the American continent certainly indicates that the Chinese made the voyage. How else could they have known the distance?

Hoei-Shin said that he and many others aboard the ships lived in terror during the crossing. Their greatest fear was that they would sail off the edge of Earth.

At the time, the Chinese believed Earth was in the shape of a cube. The cube was stationary—it didn't move. Around it, supposedly carried on heavenly winds, revolved the planets, stars, and sun. Only the top of the cube was populated, with China as the "Flower of the Center." The oceans of the world flowed outward, ending in all four directions as colossal waterfalls. To sail too close to any of them was thought to be extremely dangerous. A ship that did so was doomed. Ultimately, the ship and all aboard—the captain, crew, and passengers—would be swept over one of the monstrous falls and plunge to certain death.

Why did the Chinese call the land Fusang? Hoei-Shin explained: "Many Fusang trees grow there. The sprouts resemble those of the bamboo tree, and the people eat them.

These ships are from the Sui dynasty of the late sixth century, but they are likely similar to the vessels of Hoei-Shin's fleet.

The fruit is like a pear in form, but is red. The thorns at the ends of the leaves are used as needle and thread. From the bark they prepare a type of very soft cloth that the people use for clothing. The buds are like bamboo shoots, and the people eat them. They also grind them into a paste, which is allowed to ferment and from it an alcoholic beverage called *pulque* is brewed. . . . Paper is made using the fiber from this tree; houses are built of the wood."

The Fusang tree mentioned sounds very much like the cactuslike agave plant. Also known as the century plant (because most varieties bloom infrequently), it grows naturally only in North, South, and Central America, with the greatest concentration in Mexico.

Hoei-Shin told about the everyday life, customs, and beliefs of the early Maya. With remarkably few exceptions, his descriptions duplicate those of modern historians. All are things that could have been known only by being there.

Of the Mayan towns and cities he had visited, Hoei-Shin said that the people were peaceful and more interested in building and improving their lives than engaging in warfare. He said the people's dwellings were made of wooden beams and a mixture of water, clay, and grass (adobe), and many had roofs of tile but of a different style than those in China (which had flared eaves). Also, unlike China, the Mayan cities were not enclosed by walls.

Hoei-Shin also learned about the prison system of Fusang. "The country has two prisons," he explained. "One is in northern Fusang, the other is in the south.

Ordinary criminals are put in the southern prison. Those convicted of serious crimes are sent to the northern one. Prisoners in the southern jail can be pardoned. Those in the northern jail are there for life. [However], they are allowed to marry. Their offspring become slaves, boys at age eight and girls at nine."

As for the marriage customs of the people, Hoei-Shin said, "A man seeking a wife builds a house in front of the girl's home (or that of her parents) and lives in it. He cleans and waters the grounds of her house in the mornings and evenings. After a year, if she is not satisfied with him, he is driven away; if she is pleased, they marry."

Modern day historians specializing in the study of early Mexico say that this was how a man would go about seeking a wife. Based on studies of Mayan picture writing, the historians' findings echo the words of Hoei-Shin.

The Chinese claim that they discovered America before Columbus first came to light in the Western world in 1761. In that year, French historian J. de Guignes published *Chinese Voyages to the American Coast*, a book about the travels of Hoei-Shin

This panel is from the sixth-century Mayan Temple of the Sun in Palenque, Mexico. In the eighteenth century, a man named Antonio de Solis discovered the ruins of the Mayan city of Palenque. On an inside wall was a well-preserved mural, one panel of which shows two men exchanging gifts. The strangest and most important detail of the picture is that one of the men (at right) has a pigtail—a long braid of hair hanging at the back of the head. Mayan men did not wear their hair in this way. The style is uniquely Chinese.

and others in the New World. Yao Silian's writings about the subject provided de Guignes with the basic information he needed.

De Guignes had no way of knowing it, but Hoei-Shin's journey is not the whole story of Chinese contact with Mexico and other foreign lands. In fact, it is only the beginning. In 1421 a fleet of almost two hundred ships under the command of Admiral Zheng He set sail from China on a monumental voyage of discovery. During the expedition, they not only reached the Americas but also Australia, New Zealand, Africa, the Caribbean, Antarctica, and Greenland.

Chinese ships of the time were by far the largest and most skillfully constructed in the world. Up to 400 feet (122 m) in length, made of teak bound with iron, they were flat bottomed, rectangular in shape, and multistoried. Oarsmen and massive square sails of red silk powered them, and watertight compartments provided protection against sinking.

The captains of such ships had the knowledge and tools necessary to make voyages across the vast Pacific. In addition to a compass to show their direction, they had maps and nautical devices for determining their position at sea.

The ships traveled in large convoys, protected by warships at the points of a diamond-shaped formation. In the center of the formation were supply ships, passenger ships, and other vessels of various kinds.

In 1421 a towering man named Zheng He (holding scroll) commanded the Ming dynasty's fleet of immense trading vessels on the first of what would be seven expeditions ranging as far as Africa and the Americas.

THE USE OF JADE FOR BURIAL ATTIRE

In fifth-century China, when a wealthy or important person died, pieces of jade were placed in the deceased's mouth. Doing so, it was believed, gave the individual immortality—eternal life. So strong was this belief that the bodies of some royal persons were laid to rest wearing jade masks. Some were even buried wearing suits made entirely of jade. There is only one place other than China where such unique burial attire was worn by the dead: Mexico.

This Jade mosaic mask (left) was made for Lord Pacal, seventh century ruler of Palenque, Mexico.

The Jade funeral suit of Princess Tou Wan (below), Han dynasty, is from the late second century B.C.

On large Chinese ships of the 1400s, as many as two hundred slaves rowed oars, said to be as big as a ship's mast. At each oar, two teams of up to five men stood facing one another. Using rope handholds attached to the oar, in alternating fashion, half the men pushed and then the other half pulled. In shackles and chained to the ship, the slaves often worked nonstop at a numbing pace.

Thousands of horses for the Chinese cavalry were carried on specially designed ships. The horses were kept in stables and tended to around the clock by crew members, who fed them mashed boiled rice and filled their troughs with water, up to 3 gallons (11 liters) of water per horse per day.

Having a sufficient supply of water for the crew and animals was a major concern. To meet this need, seawater was made drinkable using desalinating equipment. And whenever the convoy made a stop, wooden kegs were filled with freshwater from streams and lakes.

The supply ships carried charcoal, extra timbers, replacement parts, and large quantities of rice, beans, and other foodstuffs. Livestock such as chickens, hogs, and goats, kept in pens and cages on deck, were brought for milking or slaughtering during the journey. Edible and ornamental plants were grown in pots on deck. Frogs were bred in large vats.

Everyone in the armada had well-defined roles, including mapmakers who charted newly discovered lands, historians who recorded details of the voyage, and monks who provided spiritual guidance and went ashore with landing parties to spread Buddhist gospel.

The first part of the armada's route took it southward to the Philippines and Indonesia and then westward to India, all countries the Chinese had visited many times before. From India the armada sailed south to Australia and New Zealand, northwest around the cape of Africa, then across the Atlantic to eastern North America. From there it sailed down through the Caribbean, around South

America, then up along western Mexico, the United States, Canada, and Alaska. Finally, the armada headed for home across the Pacific.

The evidence supporting the claim of Chinese visits to these lands is substantial:

Antiquities collector Liu Gang unveiled this map in January 2006, claiming it proves that Chinese seafarer Zheng He sailed to America more than seventy years before Christopher Columbus arrived. A note on the map says that it was made in 1763 as a copy of an original drawn in 1418. The map does indeed depict North America and even Antarctica, but scholars remain skeptical of the map's validity.

AUSTRALIA

* Several anchors of Chinese design have been found off the coast, as have large quantities of broken Chinese ceramics.
* Chinese naval officers wore red, robelike uniforms. In 1838 archaeologists found a cave in which there is a picture of a man clothed in a red garment reaching to his ankles.
* In 1862 a man named John Green saw a Chinese junk rise from the sea following a storm.
* The fleets collected animals from foreign lands, including kangaroos. These animals, unique to Australia, were displayed in the Imperial Zoo in Beijing.

CARIBBEAN

* Columbus met Chinese people when he arrived in Cuba and reported that he had found Chinese bodies in the Azores, a string of islands in the Atlantic Ocean that runs between 1,200 and 2,400 miles (1,900 and 3,800 km) off the eastern coast of North America.

NATIVE AMERICANS

Recently, scientists have studied the DNA of the native populations of North, South, and Central America. Their analyses show conclusively that some of the people of Mexico, Panama, Colombia, Venezuela, and Peru, for example, have some DNA markers similar to those of the Chinese. Many archaeologists believe that this is further evidence of Chinese voyages to the Americas. To a degree, they are probably right. However, more likely it is proof of something altogether different—and more important.

It has long been believed that roughly twenty-five thousand years ago, during Earth's most recent ice age, a lowering of the sea level made it possible to travel from Asia to America on foot. Over the centuries, Asian people migrated slowly south—and southeast—down through what is now Alaska, Canada, the United States, Mexico, and Central and South America. Intermarriage between Chinese explorers and native peoples could explain the similarities in DNA markers, but only to a very limited extent. However, an Asian migration would *fully* explain why this genetic fingerprint is everywhere in the Americas.

NORTH AMERICA (EAST COAST)

* The earliest European settlers in this part of the world found trees and plants native to China.
* Sixteenth-century Italian explorer Giovanni da Verrazano reported finding Chinese people in what is modern day New York.
* Friends of George Washington discovered the remains of a Chinese junk when a swamp was drained on his property.

SOUTH AMERICA

* The wrecks of Chinese ships have been found off the coast of Chile.
* Chickens of a breed once exclusive to Asia are found in abundance in many South American countries.
* The name *Peru* is a Chinese word meaning "white mist." Nearly one hundred villages in Peru have Chinese names, and in two of these, the people could, until a century ago, communicate in Chinese.
* Many pieces of Incan pottery bearing Chinese writing have been found throughout western South America.

CENTRAL AMERICA AND MEXICO

* Several early European explorers reported finding Chinese people in Central America and Mexico.

These Mayan clay figurines are dated ca. A.D. 700–1000. Their facial features have many Asian characteristics.

* Throughout the region, Chinese inscriptions have been discovered on stone walls, and Chinese vases, statuettes, and pictures of horses (otherwise unknown in the Americas prior to Columbus) have also been discovered.
* Chinese neck-rest pillows and carrying poles have been found in Mexico and Central America.

NORTH AMERICA (WEST COAST)

* In California, Native Americans tell of an Asian colony established before the arrival of European explorers.
* Several Chinese anchors have been found off the California coast.
* North of San Francisco, the wreck of a Chinese junk was found buried under a sandbank in the Sacramento River. Medieval Chinese armor was in its hold.
* The Squawmish Indians of Canada tell of visits by Chinese traders long ago, and to this day, the Squawmish use words identical to Chinese (for example, *tsil*, meaning "wet," and *chin*, meaning "wood").
* Thousands of ancient Chinese coins have been discovered in Canada.
* Native Americans in Alaska speak of "men dressed in long, many-colored silk clothing . . . who came [to our land long ago]. Their heads were shaved except for a tress [pigtail] on the back."

When the notion of Chinese visits to America first came to light in the eighteenth century, most people were intrigued but very skeptical. They wanted more proof. In the twenty-first century, there is more evidence than anyone could possibly have expected.

GREENLAND

ICELAND

A.D. 900-1100

Labrador

Sculpin
Island

Newfoundland

NORTH AMERICA

IRELAND

EUROPE

ATLANTIC OCEAN

AFRICA

SOUTH AMERICA

N

W   E

S

0   400   800 mi
0   400   800 km

CHAPTER 4
THE STRANGE FATE
OF CELI DEI

Irish

A.D. 900-1100

The Celi Dei was a large group of Christian monks who settled in Ireland around A.D. 725. They were ascetics. That is, they lived a very simple life in which material things were of no importance. Their only possessions were a wooden cross about their neck and the clothes they wore—a hooded robe and sandals. They believed that people were closest to God, not in a church but in the wilderness, communing with nature and existing in harmony with the other living creatures of Earth. Their name, literally translated, means "servants of God."

The Celi Dei ate only the most natural of foods—nuts, berries, and eggs, for example. In the beginning, they lived in caves or small huts, usually beehive-shaped structures with rounded walls of stone and sod. Though the policy would change later, originally no women were allowed near their dwellings.

By A.D. 750, the Celi Dei had begun building monasteries—huge residences for their expanding flock. For the next hundred years, they worked. During this time, from A.D. 750 to 850, the Celi Dei built monasteries throughout Ireland and on many nearby islands. To increase their numbers, they decided to take wives, fellow believers who would live and worship as they did, and also bear children who would grow to follow the same faith.

Their lives were good and peaceful. But then a group of pirate Norwegians known as Vikings arrived. In 795 the Vikings began launching bloody raids on the island and coastal monasteries of the Celi Dei. Though the monks had little money and only a few valuables, they had other things the Vikings needed: food and, even more important, ready-made castlelike residences for themselves and their families.

Every raid was a guaranteed success. As the Vikings well knew, the Celi Dei were pacifists. They believed in turning the other cheek and in loving one's enemy. They refused to fight back.

Many of the men were slaughtered and their wives and children kidnapped and enslaved. Those who escaped the Vikings fled inland, deeper into the woods of Ireland.

This left the Vikings to take over the monasteries and do as they pleased all along the coast. By 832 the Vikings had founded a series of coastal towns—Dublin, Wexford, Limerick, and others. Also, they sailed their ships up the rivers of Ireland and then placed their fleets on inland lakes. From these floating fortresses, they could attack any part of the surrounding countryside.

In their vessels, the Vikings hunted down the Celi Dei and once again began killing the men and kidnapping the women and children to be used as slaves.

The Celi Dei had no choice. For the second time, they would have to flee. In vessels called curraghs, they sailed by the hundreds to the nearest large body of land—Iceland.

Iceland received its name in 861 from one of the earliest settlers there, a Viking named Floki. He and his crew spent the summer fishing and failed to store fodder for the livestock during the winter. When winter hit, it killed all of their cattle and sheep. When Floki returned home to Norway, instead of admitting that the livestock had died because of his poor planning, he blamed the place for his misfortune and named it Iceland.

Curraghs were both strange and seaworthy little boats. Broad to the point of looking round, they were from 20 to 30 feet (6 to 9 m) in diameter. The gunwales (upper edge of the sides of the boat) were of willow. The hull was of wicker, a springy type of reed woven to form a framework. Over this framework, three layers of hides were stretched. First boiled and then tanned over an oak fire, the three layers of hardened leather gave curraghs additional thickness as well as increased buoyancy as the layers formed double air chambers. Butter and lard were used to waterproof the leather. Tar and holly resin were used as caulking. A circular leather cover, which could be raised by a tent-pole-like staff, protected the sailors and their supplies from the elements.

Oars furnished the primary source of power. Curraghs also carried a mast and a triangular leather sail. These were stowed much of the time and brought out only when the wind was strong.

In Wales, curraghs (ABOVE) *are still used to this day. The Welsh (as did the Irish Celi Dei) also used a type of boat called a coracle. Like curraghs, coracles were made of wickerwork and hides but were completely round and much smaller. The largest were big enough to carry as many as a dozen passengers, but most were so small that there was room for only one or two people.*

For heating and cooking, the curraghs carried a brazier. The voyagers burned peat moss or charcoal in this large metal container. To keep the fire from having any contact with the hides, especially those of the bottom of the boat, the brazier was suspended from a metal rod set in place between the gunwales. Water was carried in "skins" (leather bags), or in "bladder bags," containers made from the dried bladders of sheep, goats, and cows. At sea the diet of the Celi Dei consisted, for the most part, of fruit, nuts, potatoes, carrots, grain, and dried fish.

Though sturdy, curraghs were slow and difficult to steer, relying entirely on oarsmen and a sternpost rudder to keep them on course. The voyage to Iceland took months, with the Celi Dei reaching it only by making frequent stops at small North Atlantic islands where they could rest and repair and reprovision their boats.

Many of the curraghs were lost at sea. Still, several succeeded in reaching Iceland. Exhausted and near starving, the monks went ashore—and set to work making new lives for themselves. At considerable length, the Icelandic sagas (the historical written records of Iceland) tell the story of the arrival of the Celi Dei and of their establishing a colony near the seashore.

For the next seventy-five years, the colony prospered and expanded. Beehivelike homes were built. The land was farmed, the seas and lakes fished, and livestock raised. Grapes were to be found growing in the wild. New settlements were established, some on nearby islands. The women had many children. Also, monks from other orders learned of the Celi Dei's colony and decided to make the journey and join them.

> Generally, Iceland's winter climate is like that of the northern United States with an average temperature of 30° F (-1° C). Iceland's summers are colder, however, at an average temperature of 52° F (11° C).

Eric the Red's expulsion from Iceland led to his taking a group to Greenland in 982, much to the detriment of the Celi Dei, who were thriving there.

The Vikings also heard about the colonies.

Soon the striped sails and serpentine prows of Viking warships appeared on the horizon. In no time, they were ravaging the settlements of the Celi Dei (as well as those of others) in Iceland.

Once again, the Celi Dei would have to flee.

For a time, they hid, refurbishing and supplying their boats. Then, when the first opportunity presented itself, on a moonless night, they slipped away into the blackness, in the direction of Greenland.

Though Greenland's climate and terrain are actually far harsher than those of Iceland, the Celi Dei made the best of it. Ice-capped mountains dominated the huge island, but the coastal areas were fertile, and livestock and crops, especially potatoes and turnips, could be grown. By 875 they had established several thriving colonies.

For 108 years they lived in peace. Then one morning in 982, a single Viking ship was spotted. It happened to be that of Eric the Red, the father of Leif Ericsson, who had been expelled from Iceland for murder. Greenland would be his new home, he decided, and he would rule it by force.

The Celi Dei expected to be attacked immediately. But luck was with them. Though the Vikings spent the first few months exploring the country, nosing into every bay and cove, looking for the best place to settle down, they failed to spot the Celi Dei.

The monks knew, however, that it was only a matter of time before the Vikings found them. Once again, they would have to abandon their homes. They gathered their people together and set sail, headed west in yet another flotilla of curraghs. This time they truly put themselves in the hands of God. There were rumors of a great land to the west but no details of its proximity or location.

They escaped just in the nick of time. Very shortly after they'd fled, Eric discovered their abandoned homesteads. *The Book of the Icelanders,* a volume written by Icelandic historian Ari the Wise (ca. 1067–1148) states, "They [Eric and his crew] found these men's [abandoned] habitations both in [the] east and west in the land. [There were] broken hide boats and a stone smithery [metalworking shop], whereby it may be seen that the same kind of folk [Irish] had been there."

The voyage, to the surprise of the Celi Dei, was unexpectedly short: only four days. In the year 982, they landed in North America, on the desolate, rocky coast of Labrador. Only a few stayed, and they founded a small colony on a place called Sculpin Island. The rest continued on, hugging the coast in their curraghs in search of a suitable place for a new colony. They found many, but they discovered that the farther south they traveled, the more inviting the land became.

It is believed that they came to what is modern day Massachusetts and began sailing up the Merrimack River, no doubt thrilled by the temperate climate and the beauty of the land through which they were traveling. When they reached what is now the town of Haverhill, New Hampshire, they came ashore.

Exploring the new land, the Celi Dei made their way along a Native American trail.

> *Greenland was discovered by Europeans for the first time in 872 by a Norwegian Viking named Gunnbjorn Ulfsson and was first known as Gunnbjorn's Land.*

They came to a place of rolling meadows and lush green forests. And beyond that there was a peculiar sort of area, one where structures had been made using large slabs of stone. By accident, the Celi Dei had arrived at Pattee's Caves, now known as America's Stonehenge, the site of the Phoenician colony of one thousand years before.

They quickly set to clearing the caves and making them habitable. One was converted into a chapel. Near the caves, fifteen beehive-shaped homes of rock were built, and over time, more structures were erected, of timber, sod, and stone.

The Celi Dei had never been happier. The rivers were full of fish, the woods with game, and the land was fertile. Grapes, berries, and other foods grew in abundance in the wild.

From the outset, the relations between the Celi Dei and the native people of the region, the Algonquin, were cordial. Though these wandering people probably looked strange to the Algonquin, the Celi Dei were friendly, humble, and posed no threat. They did not carry any sort of weapon. And perhaps most importantly, the monks and their families did not want to take or change the land. They simply wanted to coexist with it and their neighbors.

Soon the Native Americans were showing the Celi Dei the use of traps for hunting and fishing. Also, they tutored them in the planting and cultivation of maize and other crops. On their part, the Celi Dei showed the Algonquin how to grow and harvest potatoes, turnips, and oats.

In time, the Celi Dei began establishing settlements throughout New England, often erecting structures made of stacked slabs of stone, all constructed in a Celtic style of crude architecture they'd used in Great Britain and Europe. The new settlements became the largest and busiest of all and came to be called Great Ireland.

The Celi Dei communities were thriving. But then, like a recurring nightmare, a speck appeared on the horizon. Slowly, it grew larger and its form more distinct—until all was clear: once more, the striped sail of a Viking ship was headed toward their sanctuary. Soon the bloody men of the north would again be upon them.

This time the Celi Dei elected to fight. For more than two centuries they had been butchered and pillaged by the Vikings. Again and again, they had run from the vicious pagans. But now, the Celi Dei knew, they could run no farther. They had found a home they loved. And this time, they would fight to the death for it.

The Celi Dei and their Algonquin friends armed themselves with bows and arrows, tomahawks, and heavy cudgels. They boarded hidden curraghs and watched and waited.

They did not have to wait long.

The Viking ship eased into the river and began heading up it. As it came within striking distance, the Celi Dei and the Algonquin attacked.

Releasing anger built up through centuries of fear and anguish, the warrior monks and their allies tore into the Vikings ferociously. Taken completely by surprise, the Norsemen were soundly defeated. How many of them were killed and injured is not recorded, nor are the losses suffered by the Celi Dei and their allies.

The survivors were taken prisoner. Their ship was set on fire and destroyed, and they were forbidden to ever leave. This last stricture was especially important to the Celi Dei: If even a single prisoner were able to return to his homeland, the haven of the Celi Dei would be known. In short order, more Viking marauders would descend on them. To further prevent their escape, the Celi Dei forcibly baptized them all Christians. And then, as Christians, they were ordered to vow that they would never try to escape.

Only when it was over, when they became better able to communicate with their captives, did the Celi Dei discover the dark irony of the ugly episode.

The leader of the Viking group, a man named Ari Mason, believed in peace, equality, and brotherly love. Though of Viking heritage, he was merely a trader, not a pirate. He had long heard of the Celi Dei and admired them and their values. When at first, he had seen the numerous curraghs descending the river, Ari had been thrilled by what he thought was a large welcoming party for him and his crew.

The Celi Dei were ashamed and wracked with guilt over what they had done. They had broken their own covenant, their own law: they had taken up arms against their fellow human. And by a darkly illuminating twist of fate, the first time they had done so, it turned out that the persons they had attacked had been friends.

How do we know this story? How do we know all these details about an Irish settlement in eastern North America that existed more than one thousand years ago?

Round, beehive-shaped houses of stacked stone have been discovered throughout New England. These dwellings are identical to those found in one other part of the world—Ireland. Also, New Hampshire's Pattee's Caves, thought to have been constructed one thousand years before by the Phoenicians, were clearly occupied by a second group of voyagers to the New World. These people remodeled the strange habitation and converted some of the rooms into what appear to be Christian chapels.

In 1529 a map showing the 1524-1528 travels of Italian navigator Giovanni da Verrazano was published, one in which Great Ireland is clearly identified. Other maps

Round, beehived-shaped houses, such as those shown here, are commonly found in Ireland. Similar structures have been found throughout New England.

showing the Irish settlements were drawn by Flemish explorer Gerhardus Mercator in 1541 and by English explorer Sir Humphrey Gilbert in 1582.

Historian Charles Boland states, "That such a place as Great Ireland existed is beyond doubt. It is a fact set down in the Icelandic sagas." These include *Hauk's Book* (named for its author), the *Islendingabok* (Book of the Icelanders), and the *Landnamabok* (Book of Settlements). All these works detail the origins of the Celi Dei in Ireland and their fleeing the Vikings, first to Iceland, then to Greenland, and finally to Great Ireland in northeast America. "[There]," wrote Boland, "the monks settled down into the routine life . . . their emotions could have betrayed naught but joy. The woods were filled with game . . . the Merrimack [River] swarmed with fish, [and] the Indians could supply them with knowledge."

What became of the Celi Dei? Perhaps many assimilated with Native Americans. At least one large contingent set off to establish new settlements and spread their beliefs to other parts of the world (as you will read about in Chapter 8). And not a few returned home, to Iceland, Greenland, and northern Europe. By the beginning of the eleventh century, the Celi Dei had ceased to exist in New England.

GREENLAND

ICELAND

Gunnbjorn's
Skerry

A.D. 986

NORWAY

Labrador

NORTH AMERICA

Newfoundland

Nova
Scotia

EUROPE

ATLANTIC OCEAN

AFRICA

N

W   E

S

SOUTH AMERICA

0   300   600 mi

0   300   600 km

CHAPTER 5
THE TIMID VIKINGS

Vikings
A.D. 986

The Vikings kept fairly detailed accounts—both oral and written—of their adventures and explorations. Most often the records were in the form of sagas of important Nordic people. One such person was Bjarni Herjulfsson. Though he was a huge, powerfully built man, Bjarni Herjulfsson wasn't terribly curious or brave.

Born in the middle of the tenth century in Iceland, Bjarni Herjulfsson grew up to become a trader. Thus, the vessel he captained was a cargo ship, a type known by Vikings as a *knorr*. Though sturdy, it was far less colorful than a Viking warship.

Viking warships were known as *langskips* (longships) or *dreki* (dragon ships). They were elegantly painted and sported grotesque figureheads of huge wooden dragons or serpents. They employed a single large woolen sail, often striped and

A Viking vesssel from ca. 800, showing the single sail and carved prow typical of the longships.

emblazoned with stags or other symbols of physical prowess. Usually 120 feet (37 m) in length, a warship's complement of up to fifty soldiers alternated at the oars. Around the gunwale the Vikings often hung brightly colored shields. The gunwales were unusually broad—broad enough to walk on—to make boarding (and capturing) other ships easier.

By comparison, a knorr was not quite so impressive. The vessel was shorter than a langskip, its sides were higher, and it was much wider—almost fat-looking. There was no intricately carved figurehead. In

The Vikings ships known as knorrs (model above) *were made for long, deep water voyages.*

fact, the entire craft was undecorated. Painted only above the waterline, the bottom was coated with seal tar to protect against worms. Its single mast carried a striped woolen sail. Its oars were used only for maneuvering into and out of port or when the wind failed. Steering was achieved by use of a large steering oar, in the stern (rear) of the ship on the starboard (right) side. Such vessels typically had a crew of thirty. Each sailor was given a sea chest in which to keep his belongings. The chest doubled as a rowing seat.

When sailing near land, Vikings beached their vessel for the night and went ashore to stretch their legs, rest, and have a hot meal. Campfires were lit, and soup and stew were cooked in cauldrons suspended over the flames. Wood-framed tents were set up. For the leaders of the expedition, there were travel beds, but the crew slept in two-person skin bags that had been filled with tools and other gear during the daytime.

Once the Vikings headed into open, uncharted ocean, the hardships really began. Icebergs smashed hulls. Ferocious, bitterly cold storms raged. There were no cabins of any kind and no protection from the elements except for tent canvas or oiled skins stretched over part of the ship. Privacy did not exist. The only way to go to the bathroom was over the side, the gunwale.

On the voyages, the people were cold, wet, and miserable most of the time. Because no fires were allowed aboard a ship, the food was always cold. Adding to everyone's discomfort, it was extremely crowded—not only with sailors and settlers but also with equipment and supplies. On cargo vessels, there was the added crunch of livestock—sheep, pigs, poultry, and so forth—and mounds of trading goods, including lumber.

It was in such a vessel that Bjarni Herjulfsson, in 986, traveled from his native Iceland to Norway. After unloading passengers and cargo, Bjarni Herjulfsson returned home, only to find out that his father—Herjulf—had decided to leave the country and go to Greenland without him. Bjarni Herjulfsson decided to go in search of his father—despite the fact that Bjarni Herjulfsson didn't know where Greenland was. All he knew was that it was to the west somewhere and that its interior consisted mostly of tall mountains and glaciers. He told his crew: "Our voyage must be regarded as foolhardy, seeing that no one of us has ever been in the Greenland Sea."

On their third day at sea, a storm hit. As the Icelandic sagas tell it, "They set out to sea, and the fair winds ceased. Storms [overtook them] and northern winds with fog

> *The Vikings came from what are now the Scandinavian countries of Norway, Sweden, and Denmark. They were known by many other names: Norsemen, Northmen, Russ, Varangians, and Danes. Not until the nineteenth century did historians begin calling them Vikings.*

blew continually, so that for many days they did not [even] know in what direction they were sailing."

Because of the storm, Bjarni Herjulfsson and his crew sailed right past Greenland, straight toward America.

According to the sagas: "[After many days] they approached land and saw that it was flat and covered with woods, and there were small hillocks upon it . . . the sailors said that they thought it best to land for [they had been many days at sea] . . . and lacked both food and water, but Bjarni Herjulfsson did not want to land, and said they had enough left. At this, the men grumbled somewhat."

For Bjarni Herjulfsson not to have made landfall, especially if they were low on supplies, makes no sense. Not only did they need provisions, but the crew needed a rest. Also, stopping might have helped Bjarni Herjulfsson get some idea as to where they were (which was possibly on one of the small Atlantic islands known as Gunnbjorn's Skerry).

The Vikings, with their sailing skill, ruled the North Atlantic from A.D. 800 to 1050.

Regardless, big Bjarni Herjulfsson just kept going, headed west.

Three days later, he and his crew again spotted land—a great mass of it, the seemingly endless coastline of a new continent. What the captain and crew were seeing was the eastern coast of what would come to be known as North America. According to the sagas, "[The men again] asked Bjarni Herjulfsson if he would like to go ashore there, and he replied that he would not do so as the land had an 'inhospitable look.'"

If the men "grumbled somewhat" the first time Bjarni Herjulfsson wouldn't land, they must have been near mutiny when he did it again. The crew, at this point, had been at sea for ten days and nights and was exhausted. The supply of food and water had reached a critical point. And last but certainly not least, it was obvious to everyone on board that they had reached a whole new world. It was not only traditional—but expected—of a Viking captain to explore any new lands discovered.

Originally, the word VIKING *described an action, not a person. To go* A-VIKING *meant "to sail off on a raiding party."*

By saying that the land looked "inhospitable," Bjarni Herjulfsson was basically saying that it looked unfriendly and dangerous and that he was afraid to land.

That the crew didn't mutiny may be due to their own fears. As it's been said, Bjarni Herjulfsson was an especially powerful man—and the consequences of defying the behemoth could prove to be very painful. In short, the crew was afraid of him. Also, the men may have been as incurious and scared of the new continent as Bjarni Herjulfsson was.

No one knows. The sagas give no further details about the matter. They tell only that Bjarni Herjulfsson turned tail and headed east, back in the direction of Greenland. Incredibly, he not only found the island, but he practically docked on his father's doorstep. By accident, Bjarni Herjulfsson found his father's settlement in the first bay that he came to in Greenland.

It took a while, but Bjarni Herjulfsson eventually got around to mentioning that he had found a new continent. And eventually he had to admit he hadn't even gone ashore.

Lots of snickering went on behind Bjarni Herjulfsson's back—about "Bjarni the Brave" and so forth. Still, unwittingly, the strangely timid Viking accomplished something important. His story reached the ears of Leif Ericsson, a young man who wasn't afraid to explore the vast, new, "inhospitable-looking" land.

GREENLAND

ICELAND

Baffin
Island

Brattahlid

Gunnbjorn's
Skerry

A.D. 1003

Labrador

Vinland

L'Anse aux Meadows

Newfoundland
Gulf of St. Lawrence

NORTH AMERICA

ATLANTIC OCEAN

NORWAY

EUROPE

AFRICA

SOUTH AMERICA

N

W   E

S

0   300   600 mi
0   300   600 km

CHAPTER 6 LEIF ERICSSON

Vikings
A.D. 1003

Leif Ericsson, born in Iceland around 965, was the eldest of three brothers. As was traditional for Viking boys, at the age of eight, he was sent to live outside the family. For the next four years, he stayed at the home of a German named Thyrker, a slave taken by his father in a raid. Thyrker taught Leif how to read and write and to speak German, Russian, and Irish. He told him many of the sagas of the Vikings, and taught him about plant life, trading, and the use of weapons. Leif returned home when he was twelve, the age at which a Viking boy became a man.

When Leif was in his late teens, his father, known as Eric the Red, killed several men during a murderous quarrel. At his trial, he was declared an outlaw and exiled from Iceland for three years. In the spring of 981, he and his family sailed west for the group of islets known as Gunnbjorn's Skerry. Blown off course, Eric missed the place by a few hundred miles

Eric the Red, father of Leif Ericsson, is shown attacking an Icelandic chief, part of an incident for which he was banished from Iceland.

and ended up being the first Viking to find Greenland—preceding Bjarni Herjulfsson's father by five years.

After three years in the frigid wasteland, Leif returned with his father to Iceland. His father, a huckster through and through, gave Greenland its lush, verdant-sounding name and talked more than five hundred people into paying him to lead them in colonizing the large island he'd discovered.

In 984 twenty-five Viking ships departed for Greenland. Again and again, monstrous storms tore into the convoy.

Only fourteen of the twenty-five ships reached Greenland. Some were driven back to Iceland and the rest lost at sea. Only about three hundred people out of the original five hundred survived the journey.

Greenland, the world's largest island, is far colder than Iceland. Its average winter temperature is -21°F (-29° C). Its average in the summer is 50°F (10°C). More than four-fifths of the land is covered with permanent ice.

When the ships finally ground ashore, the settlers were horrified by what they saw. Greenland was nothing but a massive ice cap with only a fringe of green around the coast. And it was far colder and more barren than the homes they'd left behind in Iceland. The settlers knew they'd been duped, but there wasn't much they could do except make the best of it.

Eric rightfully claimed to be the Viking founder of Greenland. But it wasn't long before he also proclaimed himself to be the *ruler* of the country. This was more than a lot of the people could take. They wanted no part of Eric and certainly had no intention of being ruled by him. A group of almost a hundred headed up the Greenland coast and established what became known as the Western Settlement. Meanwhile, at the original Eastern Settlement, Eric announced that his farm, at a place called Brattahlid (meaning "Steep Slope"), was the country's capital.

It was at Brattahlid that Leif, his two brothers, and his half sister, Freydis, grew up. During the long winters, when it often stayed dark twenty-four hours a day, there was little to do but take care of the livestock and try to stay warm. During the summers, everything was reversed. The sun shone around the clock and temperatures reached 60°F (16°C). Leif and his brothers hunted, fished, and helped plant and harvest crops. And whenever they had free time, they went off exploring.

After several years at Brattahlid, Leif's father asked him to sail to Norway to pay his respects to the king. Leif gathered a crew of fourteen, including his mentor and teacher, Thyrker, and sailed east. Only twenty-four years old, he captained the langskip across the Atlantic, first to Iceland and then to Norway, where he and his men stayed for the winter. Olaf II, the king of Norway, granted Leif an audience, which resulted in the two men becoming fast friends. The two played chess, and they talked. Often, King Olaf spoke of Christianity. Before leaving Norway, Leif and all of his men were baptized and confirmed in the faith.

When he returned to Greenland, Leif brought a priest with him. Soon many Greenlanders were converting to the new religion, including Leif's mother. But his

> Greenland is only 175 miles (282 km) away from Iceland and is visible from that country's western mountaintops.

Eric the Red established his family compound (left) known as Brattahlid in southwestern Greenland in the late tenth century. His descendants were believed to have lived there for more than five hundred years.

61

red-haired father wanted no part of it—until his wife demanded that he build a small chapel on his property. If he didn't, she swore she would have nothing more to do with him.

Eric built the chapel but never set foot in the completed building.

In 999 Leif heard the story of Bjarni Herjulfsson, the "timid Viking" who had seen a new continent but had never set foot on it. Leif decided he would undertake an expedition to the new land. He went to see Bjarni Herjulfsson, learned as much as he could from him about how to reach the continent, and then bought Bjarni Herjulfsson's ship on the spot. So many Vikings wanted to be part of the adventure that most had to be turned away.

Leif asked his father if he would lead the expedition. Eric wasn't at all eager and protested that he was too old and feeble for such an undertaking. But Leif persisted until his father finally agreed.

On the day they were to depart, gray-haired Eric mounted his horse and headed down the trail to where the ship was being readied for launching. Suddenly his horse stumbled and went down, throwing Eric and injuring his side and leg. Not only was he hurt, but it was also a strongly held Viking superstition that such an accident was the worst of omens for a journey—it forewarned of disaster for all. According to the sagas, Eric told Leif, "It is not designed for me to discover more lands than the one in which we are now living, nor can we now continue longer together."

Undeterred by the omen, Leif and a crew of thirty-five men departed Greenland in the summer of 1003 and headed into the unknown. He knew nothing about the land except for the recollections and crude drawings of Bjarni Herjulfsson, which showed the course of his return trip to Greenland.

Following Bjarni Herjulfsson's route in reverse, Leif sailed west—and after only four

In her old age, Leif's mother became a nun and a recluse.

days at sea, he sighted what is now part of North America. Most likely, he was off the coast of northeastern Canada, near a place called Baffin Island.

According to the Viking sagas, "They sailed up to the land and cast anchor, and launched a boat and went ashore." In so doing, Leif Ericsson became the first known Viking explorer to set foot in America. (But he was not the first European. The Irish Celi Dei had been in America at least a century before. Also, Ari Mason and his crew, Icelanders of Nordic background, had preceded him by eleven years.)

In 1964 U.S. president Lyndon Johnson declared October 9 to be Leif Ericsson Day in the United States to honor Ericsson and his men (as depicted above) for having been the first Vikings to set foot on American soil.

Because the place seemed to be nothing but a huge tableland of rock, Leif named it Helluland (meaning "Flat-Rock Land").

Continuing southward down the coast, the air became warmer. The place, present-day Labrador, Canada, was thickly wooded. Thus, Ericsson named it Markland (Forest Land).

After a landing and brief stay in Markland, Leif and his men continued in a southerly direction. Two days later, they reached what is modern day New Brunswick, Canada. After a short stay on a grass-covered island, they sailed on, and rounding a cape, they found themselves entering a river that flowed out from a lake.

Leif and his men went ashore to explore. The *Greenland Saga* eloquently describes the crew's reaction: "The weather was fine. There was the dew on the grass, and the first thing they did was get some of it on their hands and put it to their lips. It seemed the sweetest thing they had ever tasted!" They found streams filled with salmon, forests filled with game, and meadows where wild grapes grew in profusion. For this reason, he called the place Vinland, or "Land of Wine."

L'Anse aux Meadows, the remains of a Viking village dating from about A.D. 1000, was discovered in 1960 at the northernmost tip of the island of Newfoundland, Canada.

The exact location of Leif's first settlement was at L'Anse aux Meadows, on the northern tip of Newfoundland, Canada. Not until 1960, when archaeologists discovered the remains of the place, was its location known and not until then did historians begin to accept that others had discovered America before Columbus.

Leif could see that Vinland offered everything future settlers could hope for. He and his men began building a base camp for the winter. While the work was under way, all lived in small, temporary huts called booths. Within a month's time, the camp was ready—a sturdy longhouse and two other buildings made of stone, sod, and timber.

Leif then divided his men into two groups. Each day, half the men would stay at the camp while the other half explored the land. He ordered them never to get separated from the group or travel so far that they couldn't get back before nightfall. Remarkably, during these explorations, not a single Native American was seen.

In the spring, Leif and his men sailed for home, the ship loaded with a cargo of grapes, growing vines, and timber. Just off the coast of Greenland, Leif spotted a ship being torn apart on a rocky islet, and clinging to the wave-whipped crags were fifteen men and women. Through his efforts and those of his crew, Leif saved all fifteen of the drowning sailors.

When the Greenlanders learned of Leif's discovery, they were thrilled. New expeditions and a permanent settlement were planned.

As for Leif, he never returned to Vinland. Instead, he remained in Greenland with his family. For finding such a wonderful place on the first try and for his bringing good fortune to the shipwrecked sailors, he was nicknamed Leif the Lucky.

After the death of his father, Eric, he became the most prominent and well-liked citizen of Greenland and it's leader. When he died, at about the age of sixty, people from all over the island came to honor him at his funeral.

GREENLAND

ICELAND

NORWAY

Baffin
Island

Brattahlid

Gunnbjorn's
Skerry

Labrador

THORVALD

Vinland

THORSTEIN

L'Anse aux Meadows

NORTH AMERICA

Gulf of
St. Lawrence

Newfoundland

EUROPE

FREYDIS THE INSANE

ATLANTIC OCEAN

AFRICA

SOUTH AMERICA

N

W   E

S

0   300   600 mi

0   300   600 km

CHAPTER 7
THE VIKING AND INDIAN WARS

Vikings
A.D. 1007-1121

After Leif Ericsson's voyage to North America in 1003, Vikings repeatedly explored and attempted to establish settlements in Vinland. They found only one thing standing in their way of creating a permanent colony—Algonquin Indians. Norsemen called them Skrellings, meaning "screechers," due to the shrieking cries they made to scare their enemies.

Three of the most tragic expeditions were those of Leif's two younger brothers, Thorvald and Thorstein, and his half sister, "Freydis the Insane." Another was that of Thorfinn Karlsefni, a wealthy Icelander who fought the biggest—and last—battle of the Viking and Indian wars.

Thorvald Ericsson

In 1007 Leif's younger brother Thorvald sailed to Vinland with a crew of thirty. The bearded, long-haired young man wanted to pick up where his brother had left off and explore more deeply into the heart of the new world.

The crossing went easily, and they were soon able to find Leif's original settlement—on the northern tip of Newfoundland near the mouth of the Saint Lawrence River.

Four years had passed, and time and weather had taken their toll on the place. Thorvald and his men went to work, repairing and refurbishing the longhouse and other buildings. They fished, hunted, and stockpiled food, hides, and other supplies. And then they waited out a long, frigid winter.

With the coming of spring, the men took to their ship and set out exploring. According to the sagas, "They found it a fair, well-wooded country. It was but a short distance from the forest to the sea." And there were "white sands, as well as great numbers of islands and shallows."

They also found something else: the first trace that other people already lived there. On an island, "they found a wooden building for the shelter of grain." The Vikings didn't know who had built the structure. All they knew was that they weren't alone.

They returned to their ship and continued upriver. Rounding a bend, they beheld three peculiar "mounds a short distance in from the shore." Swords drawn, "They went up to these, and saw that there were three [overturned] skin canoes with three men under each. They seized all of the men but one, who escaped with his canoe. They killed the eight men."

After these bloody (and mindless) executions, Thorvald and his crew continued exploring the winding rivers and waterways of the region. As they passed a wooded promontory, Thorvald thought it was so beautiful that he declared, "Here I should like to make my home."

He had no way of knowing how darkly ironic this statement would later prove to be.

At day's end, the Vikings made camp. None seemed bothered by the killings that day nor, apparently, were they worried about the one Native American who had escaped—and would certainly be quick to tell the rest of his people what had occurred. According to the sagas, the Vikings "were then so overpowered with sleep [from their long day of killing and exploring] that they could not keep awake, and all fell into a [heavy] slumber."

Just before dawn, the Native Americans attacked. Cries of warning went up from the Vikings. They scrambled for their weapons and then together fought their way back to their ship—and managed to launch it with all aboard. It seemed they had made their escape, but then "a countless number of skin canoes advanced toward them." From the shores and from the canoes a shower of arrows then rained down on the men as they fled downriver.

When the Vikings had finally outdistanced their attackers, "Thorvald enquired of his men whether any of them had been wounded, and they informed him that no one of them had received a wound. '[But] I have been wounded in my armpit,'" he told them.

As he lay dying, Thorvald told his men to return to Greenland. But before they did, to take him to that piece of land that "[just yesterday] seemed to me to offer so pleasant a dwelling place. Thus [I was speaking the truth] when I

A woodcut shows Viking expedition leader Thorvald fatally wounded by Native Americans on the coast of Canada, A.D. *1007.*

expressed the wish to abide there for a time. You shall bury me there, and place a cross at my head."

Centuries later, when Dutch and English colonists settled present-day New England, they heard many strange stories from the Native Americans. One was about a beautiful promontory of land that was taboo to their people. According to legend, a white god was buried there beneath a boulder.

When the colonists investigated, they found a large stone. On it was Viking (runic) writing and a cross. The colonists left the site undisturbed. But many years later, in 1831, a group of amateur archaeologists conducted a dig. Slowly the skeleton of a man emerged, the bones adorned with Viking ornaments—metal rings, buckles, and other items. Though the writing on the rock was too weathered to be readable, there is little doubt as to what they had found—the grave of Leif Ericsson's younger brother, Thorvald.

Thorvald's Rock—also known as the Norse Boulder—is presently in the Tuck Memorial Museum in Hampton, New Hampshire. The rock, which is housed in a well-like structure with steel bars across the top of the opening, has been the object of much controversy. Some scholars contend that there is evidence that Charles M. Lamprey, the owner of the land on which the stone was found, may have promoted the rock's story in order to stimulate tourism. Scholars are undecided about the stone's authenticity, though most feel that it is much more likely that Thorvald's remains lie to the north, in Nova Scotia.

The skeleton was taken to the Fall River Museum in Massachusetts.

For the next twelve years, it was on display, until the building was gutted by fire in 1843. The skeleton and some of the ornaments were destroyed, but not all. Before the fire, two rings had been sent to a museum in Denmark (the Royal Ethnological Museum in Copenhagen), where they were identified as authentic. They remain there to this day.

Thorstein Ericsson

When Thorvald's crew returned to Greenland, they told of their leader's death. The Ericsson family was grief-stricken, especially Thorstein, the youngest of the three brothers. He vowed to go to Vinland and retrieve his brother's body. The following summer, at the Western Settlement, he equipped the same ship used by his father and brother. Accompanied by his wife, Gudrid, and with a crew of twenty-five, Thorstein set sail for Vinland.

It was supposed to be only a four- or five-day sail. But no sooner were they out of sight of land than a monstrous storm hit.

The storm raged for days. Many of their supplies—including livestock—were swept overboard. When finally the storm abated, the battered ship had been driven so far off course that neither Thorstein nor the crew had any idea where they were.

Days turned into weeks. Still, there was no sign of land in any direction. Their storm-depleted supplies began running out. Most precious of all was their food and water, and very little remained.

During the summer days, they broiled in the sun. At night, they froze. First, their water ran out and then their food. They struggled to survive by collecting rainwater and by fishing.

All became ill and weak. From being confined in the cramped, wet boat so long, most were covered with painful sores. The flesh began to shrink from their bodies, and their bones began to show.

For more than six months they drifted in the Atlantic, the sail in tatters and the rudder broken. They had no clue as to where they were—and almost no control over the ship's direction. They resigned themselves to death. But then, with the coming of the first icy week of winter, hope came as well. On the horizon was land.

Mustering all their strength, they rowed until a bizarre truth revealed itself: they had drifted at sea for over half a year, only to find they had somehow returned to Greenland.

By nightfall they made a landing but at the Eastern Settlement—not their own in the west. Frantic, in the dark and cold, Thorstein set out to find homes for all of his shipmates. He succeeded in finding places for everyone— except himself and his wife, Gudrid.

They went back to the ship and made themselves as warm and comfortable as possible. But Thorstein, already ill, quickly worsened. In the morning, he told Gudrid he would soon be dead. He told her that he loved her and thanked her for being such a good wife to him. She soothed him and lay with him in her arms to keep him warm.

He died the next day.

The irony of it all was not lost on Gudrid. Thorstein had died trying to retrieve his brother's body. Instead, like his brother, he ended up being the only person in the crew to perish on the mission.

> Gudrid was a rather exceptional woman. After the death of her second husband, she became a nun and made a religious pilgrimage all the way from Greenland to Rome, regarded as the holy city of Christianity.

Thorfinn Karlsefni and "Freydis the Insane" (A.D. 1010–1015)

Thorfinn Karlsefni, a successful trader from Iceland, led the third expedition to America. His settlement was the largest and longest held by the Vikings, lasting three years. It was also the bloodiest—and marked the beginning of the end of the Norsemen's quest to take the land.

In the spring of 1010, Karlsefni and 160 other men and women set sail for Vinland in five ships. Among the large group was a young woman named Freydis. The half sister of the three Ericsson brothers, she was beautiful but hot tempered and considered a bit odd.

Instead of going to the original settlement (at what had become known as Leif's House), they decided to establish the colony farther south, in present-day New York, on Manhattan Island, near the mouth of the Hudson River.

Instead of a longhouse, the settlers built many booths for individual families. They posted no guards. And rather than establishing their settlement in a confined, walled area, the homes were widely scattered.

One morning, a large number of Algonquin Indians approached the homesteads in canoes. With paddles, they pounded on the sides of their boats, creating a threatening clatter.

The Vikings took to their ships and slowly approached the canoes. They made signs of peace, as did the Algonquin. The two groups then rowed to an island, a thin spit of sparsely forested land. For long, strained minutes, they stared at one another, unsure of what to do.

This fine example of a Viking helmet was discovered in 1943 in a burial mound on a farm called Gjermundbu in Haug, in central eastern Norway—thus it is known as the Gjermundbu Helmet. It dates from approximately 970 A.D.

The Vikings and the Algonquin tried to converse, but their words were just meaningless babble to one another. Finally, the native people returned to their canoes and paddled away.

Not until the following spring did the Algonquin return. Out of the dawn mist a great flotilla of canoes emerged. This time, when the Vikings and Native Americans came together, say the sagas, "They began to barter with each other. Especially did the strangers wish to buy red cloth [in exchange] for animal pelts." The Algonquin cut the red cloth into strips and made headbands of it. They also wanted the Vikings' iron weapons and tools, but Karlsefni forbid it. While all the trading was going on, Karlsefni's bull bellowed. Spooked by the sudden strange sound, the Algonquin made a hurried departure.

Three weeks later, they again appeared, in greater numbers than ever. This time, the Algonquin were heavily armed, and it could be seen that they had come to attack and plunder, not trade. As the sagas tell it, "The Skrellings were all uttering loud cries. Thereupon Karlsefni and his men took shields [and weapons] and displayed them. The Skrellings sprang from their boats, and they met them and fought together. There was a fierce shower of missiles, for the Skrellings had war-slings [bows and arrows]. The Skrellings raised up on a pole a great ball-shaped body, almost the size of a sheep's belly, and [from] this they hurled [large stones] from the pole [a catapult]. And [the stones] made a frightful noise where they fell."

After the explosive crashing of the boulders slung by the catapult, "Karlsefni and all his men [fled] up a riverbank. It seemed to them that the troop of the Skrellings was rushing towards them from every side. . . . They came to jutting crags, where they [put] up a stout resistance" but then began to retreat.

It was at this point that Freydis, Leif's half sister, entered the picture—and the battle.

The sagas tell that "Freydis came out, and seeing that Karlsefni and all his men were fleeing, she cried: 'Why do ye flee from these wretches, such worthy men as ye? Had I but a weapon, methinks I would fight better than any one of you.'

"[The men] gave no heed to her words. Freydis sought to join them but lagged behind [because she was pregnant], and Skrellings pursued her." From the hand of a dead Viking, she grabbed a sword. She fended off her pursuers and then joined the fighting, leading the attack. Mounting a rocky bit of high ground, "she stripped down her shift, and slapped her breast with the naked sword. At this the Skrellings were terrified and ran down to their boats and rowed away."

After the battle, Karlsefni praised Freydis's valor. He saw that many of the enemy lay dead. Only two Vikings had perished, but a large number had been wounded, some severely.

Though they had won the battle, Karlsefni and his people knew they were too greatly outnumbered to remain. Though "the country

Freydis leads the men in driving off the Skrellings in 1009.

thereabouts was attractive, their life would be one of constant dread and turmoil. They forthwith prepared to leave, and . . . return to their own country."

After Karlsefni, in 1014, Freydis attempted to establish a colony at Leif's original settlement. It, too, ended in disaster, but not as a result of attacks by Native Americans. Instead, it was Freydis herself who caused its tragic end.

At some point, she had begun to go insane.

Perhaps it was during the bloody battle with the Algonquin, or perhaps it was shortly afterward, when she miscarried and lost her baby. Regardless, the woman gradually plunged ever deeper into madness.

After arriving at Leif's settlement, Freydis and a group of Norwegians got into a dispute—one she settled in a horridly fiendish and bloody way. Early one morning, Freydis ran sobbing to her husband and lied that she had been attacked and beaten by the Norwegians. Immediately, the men in her group grabbed up weapons and headed to the others' camp to exact revenge. Entering the Norwegians' longhouse, they found everyone asleep in bed—five men and five women. All the men were bound, dragged from the longhouse, and—on Freydis's orders—put to death.

During the second voyage, to Leif's house, Freydis informed her husband that she was taking command of the ship and the entire expedition. A weak man, he was easily bent to her will.

Only the women remained in the longhouse. When Freydis demanded that they be executed, too, the male Vikings refused. At this, Freydis calmly picked up an axe, made her way into the place, and finished the hideous business herself.

When her husband and the others later realized what Freydis had done—that she had lied and tricked them into taking part in the slaughtering of ten innocent people—they were sickened. But when confronted with the truth, she merely laughed. She told them, "[When we return], I will contrive the death of any man who shall speak of these events. We must [say] that when we left them here [they were still alive]."

Despite her threats, when they returned to Greenland the following spring, rumor quickly spread about Freydis's treachery. A trial was held, over which her half brother Leif, as Greenland's ruler, presided. A jury found Freydis guilty of murder. Her sentence: shunning. For the rest of her natural life, no one was allowed to speak to her or acknowledge her existence in any way.

Freydis sank deeper into madness and died a few years later. As for Vinland, the Vikings turned their backs on the place. Too many terrible things had happened there, and too many had died. Though the continent was the land they had dreamed of finding, it had become a place of nightmares for them. They made no further voyages there.

> It was Freydis, not her three half brothers, who inherited her father's (and grandfather's) murderous temper.

ATLANTIC OCEAN

NORTH AMERICA

W — E (compass rose)

0   140   280 mi
0   140   280 km

Mexico

Tula

Veracruz

Gulf of Mexico

Cuba

Bahamas

CHAPTER 8
THE MAN WHO BECAME A GOD

Irish
A.D. 1010

Since they had first come to the New England area one hundred years before, the Celi Dei had greatly increased their numbers. Not only had there been many children but also quite a few Native Americans and Icelandic settlers had converted to their way of life. Early in the eleventh century A.D., according to the Icelandic sagas, a man know only as the Abbot, persuaded a large contingent to once again set off to discover other lands and spread their gospel. In ships with a Viking design and a tent-covered stern for women and children, they headed south.

Weeks later, the convoy landed in northwestern Mexico, in the Yucatan region. To the Abbot's surprise, the Aztecs, the people of the region, greeted him as a god!

By coincidence, one Aztec myth was about Quetzalcoatl, a feathered serpent who was the god of the wind and of the dawn. He was associated with the coming of light and with the color white. In addition to his guise as a plumed serpent, Quetzalcoatl could take on the form of a white man with a beard.

Although often described as a feathered serpent, the Aztec god Quetzalcoatl took on many forms as seen in this elaborate depiction.

When the Abbot, a fair-skinned man with a beard, appeared on their shores, the Aztecs were sure that he was Quetzalcoatl in his human incarnation.

At Tula, the Aztec capital, the Abbot ruled as both king and god. Repulsed to find the people's religion included human sacrifice, his first order was to forbid the practice. He said that only tortillas, snakes, flowers, incense, and butterflies could be sacrificed to the gods.

For more than ten years, the Celi Dei and Aztecs lived in peace. They worked together and they intermarried. Many of the native peoples even converted to Christianity. Throughout the region, crosses were erected and small shrines built. But then drought and famine struck. Prayers went unanswered. The Aztecs, fearing they had offended their gods, reverted to the old ways—to human sacrifice. When the Abbot protested and again attempted to put a stop to the practice, he and his followers were ordered to leave.

Leading his flock, the Abbot headed south and eventually reached a place called Choula. After a stay of many years there, he and the Celi Dei decided to continue their journey and again find new land. They sailed away to the east and were never heard from again.

Before his departure, the Abbot made a promise—one that would one day help destroy an empire. He said that he would return in the distant future, in 1519 (*Ce Atl* on the Aztec calendar). Centuries later, the Spanish explorer and conquistador Hernán Cortés appeared in Mexico—in the year 1519.

As Cortés made his way inland, he saw murals and paintings of a bearded white man wearing a black, cassocklike robe and a gold cross around his neck. Some of the native people performed the communion sacrament, the Christian ceremony of eating bread and drinking wine in remembrance of Christ. (Only the Aztecs did it a bit differently, using human blood instead of wine.) He also witnessed Aztecs performing the sacrament of baptism, done in a Catholic manner, with the child being touched on the head and lips with water and given a name. Cortés wrote in his diary that Mexico was already a partly

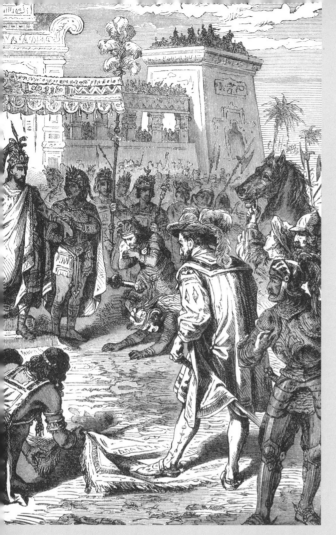

Even though welcomed as a god by the Aztecs, Cortés killed and enslaved thousands of them, eventually destroying their civilization. The image shows Cortés meeting with the Aztec emperor Montezuma, in Mexico in 1519.

Christian country when he first arrived there and wondered how such a thing could have come to be. He had no way of knowing it, but what he was seeing were remnants of the visit by the Abbot and the Celi Dei.

Because, by coincidence, Cortés arrived in 1519, the Aztecs believed he was Quetzalcoatl, the serpent god, in his earthly form, making good on his promise to come back to them in that year.

But Cortés was surely no god. Nor was he at all like the basically kind and well-intentioned Abbot. Instead, he was a greedy and ruthless man, intent on taking their land and riches by force. Too late, the Aztecs realized they had opened their doors to their conqueror and destroyer. Before the end of the next decade, most of Mexico was in the grip of the Spanish, and many of the native people were either dead or enslaved.

Buildings and temples were torn down and churches erected in their place. Books and records—written on scrolls of coarse paper—were burned. In short order, the Spanish destroyed most of the history of Mexico. Only piece by piece is it being put back together.

One fascinating chapter of Mexican history tells of the sudden appearance in Mexico in the eleventh century of a light-skinned man the people called Ce Acatl Topilzin, whom the Aztecs regarded as Quetzalcoatl. He became the king and high priest of the city of Tula and led the people to become civilized. As to what became of Ce Acatl, oral history has it that warlike factions of the region drove him into exile. He left, sailing eastward, and promised his return in 1519 on the European calendar. In virtually every aspect, this story mirrors that of the Abbot of the Celi Dei.

GREENLAND
ICELAND
ATLANTIC OCEAN
NORTH AMERICA
WALES
Lundy Island
Aber-Kerrick Gwynyon
EUROPE
Gulf Stream
Ohio River
Missouri R.
Mississippi River
Canaries Current
Bahamas
Cuba
North Equatorial Current
AFRICA
Honduras
SOUTH AMERICA
N
W
E
S
0
300
600 mi
0
300
600 km

CHAPTER 9
PRINCE MADOC OF WALES

Welsh

A.D. 1171

Born around the year A.D. 1134, Prince Madoc was one of nineteen children of Owain, the ruler of Wales. Home for Madoc—and much of the rest of his extremely large family—was Dolwyddelan Castle, a box-shaped stone fortress guarding a mountain pass.

When Owain died in December 1169, his sons began fighting over who would rule the land. Madoc wanted no part of the squabbling. And neither did his brother Riryd. Together, the two left the castle, looking to make their own way in the world.

Reaching the coastal village of Aton, they heard familiar stories of Irish and Viking voyages to a new continent across the Atlantic. The brothers decided they would do the same and purchased two ships, the *Gwennan Gorn* and *Pedr Sant*. Most likely, they were curraghs but somewhat larger than the rounded vessels of cured hide that were used by the Celi Dei. These two

In 1169 Prince Madoc fled his family home, Dolwyddelan Castle in Wales, to escape the chaos following his father's death. Although most of the building is in ruins, the keep (the central tower) was restored in the mid-nineteenth century.

were up to 40 feet (12 m) in length and capable of carrying up to thirty people. Though slow, these coracles were strong and seaworthy.

In 1170, after many weeks at sea, evidence show that Madoc and the others made landfall on the shores of present-day Alabama and settled in what is modern day Mobile Bay. The land was beautiful, warm, and fertile. As it had to the Vikings, it seemed to be completely uninhabited.

Medieval texts indicate that Prince Madoc's expedition, shown here leaving Wales, landed at the present-day location of Mobile Bay, Alabama, in 1170.

The nails used in constructing Welsh vessels in the twelfth century were made of stag's horn instead of iron. Supposedly, this prevented them from being thrown off course by the powerful attraction of "magnetic islands."

✳   ✳   ✳   ✳

Until the twenty-first century, the story of Madoc was considered little more than a legend based on fact. Why? From the fifteenth to the nineteenth centuries, Britain and Spain had many disputes over American territory. The Spanish accused the British of making up the story of Madoc in order to lay claim to the land.

The new arrivals built a rustic settlement consisting mostly of round huts. When the work was completed, Madoc decided to bring even more settlers to what he hoped would someday become a large, thriving community. Taking only his best sailors, he returned to Wales. Soon, Madoc had talked more than three hundred men, women, and children into joining him in settling the lush, inviting new land.

By year's end, leading an expedition of ten ships, Madoc returned to the settlement at Mobile Bay. The colonists then headed north, up the Alabama River—and the many waterways through middle America—very likely going ashore in what today are the states of Georgia, Tennessee, Kentucky, and Ohio. As they traveled deeper into the country, it became very clear that the Cherokee and other tribes already populated the land.

Native Americans tell the story from their perspective of the arrival of white people. Chief Oconostota of the Cherokee, as head of that nation for sixty years during the eighteenth century, said, "It is handed down by the Forefathers that . . . white people formerly inhabited the country. They were fair of skin and hair, which was brown, yellow, or red. The men had beards. I have heard my grandfather say they were a people called the Welsh, and that they had crossed the Great Water and landed first near the mouth of the Alabama River."

The Welsh settled along the banks of the Ohio River. At first, they lived in peace with the Native Americans, most of whom were

Cherokee. But then friction developed between them. The whites accused the native peoples of thievery. At the same time, the native peoples condemned the whites for taking their land and trespassing on their hunting and fishing grounds. A few isolated skirmishes slowly escalated into all-out warfare.

When a large confederacy of tribes banded together, the Welsh retreated into fortresses of stone and heavy timber. Repeatedly, the Cherokee attacked. Repeatedly they were repulsed.

The conflict continued off and on for years. Finally, under siege and near starvation, in 1186 the remaining Welsh tried to escape by fleeing downriver in curraghs. Quickly spotted by the Cherokee and their allies, they were attacked from the riverbanks— fired at with bow and arrow—and pursued by warriors in birchbark canoes. Looking for a defensible position, the Welsh ground to a stop on Sand Island, a narrow strip of land near present-day Muscle Shoals, Alabama. The place offered little refuge. From canoes Native Americans swarmed ashore and attacked. Whites were slaughtered in such numbers that their bodies lay in great heaps. The battle is said by the Indians to have gone on for days.

Finally, to prevent further bloodshed, a truce was called. The surviving Welsh were banished from the land and told never to return. By ship and on foot, they made their

Writing in 1908, scholar Reuben Durrett stated that, according to local tradition, numerous skeletons and various artifacts have, over the centuries, been dug up on Sand Island, Alabama. Some of the skeletons wore armor and helmets, and near them were weapons and shields. What happened to the items? A collection of the armor in Ohio was destroyed in a nineteenth-century fire. Most likely, Native Americans took the rest of the pieces. Supporting this contention, several explorers of the Ohio region during the sixteenth century reported seeing Indians wearing bronze armor.

way northward on the Missouri River. It is widely believed that, in what is modern day North Dakota, they became a part of a Native American group, the Mandan Indians.

Who were the Mandan? How do we know that many are, to varying degrees, the descendants of explorers from Wales?

The similarity of the round-top huts of the Mandan Indians to the houses of the first Welsh settlers in Mobile Bay is striking. The Mandans also fashioned round, coradelike sailing vessels such as those found in Wales.

During the seventeenth and eighteenth centuries, settlers told numerous tales of encounters with the Mandan, the "white Indians" of North America. For instance, in October 1792, a French fur trader named Jacques d'Eglise told of his coming upon a "remarkable tribe," many of whom were whites. D'Eglise said they were about five thousand in number and lived in ... "eight fortified villages [that] were like cities compared with other native settlements."

At first, according to d'Eglise and others, some Mandan were entirely of white heritage. Later, they intermarried with native peoples and, over time, looked more like them. By the nineteenth century, only a small number of the Mandan showed Caucasian features that might be typical of the Welsh—things such as light skin; blond or red hair; and blue, gray, or green eyes.

Recently, the papers of a Welsh missionary to North America, the Reverend Morgan Jones, were discovered. He states that in 1668, he and several members of his party were captured by a tribe of white Tuscaroras called the Doeg. As his friends were slaughtered, Jones prayed loudly in Welsh, begging God for deliverance. At the sound of his hysterical words, the white native peoples suddenly stopped. And then they responded to him in Welsh! The explorers and Indians then began to converse freely in their common language, and it was decided by tribal council to spare the remaining men. Jones lived with the Doeg for several months

One day in May 1819, a Welshman named Joseph Roberts happened to meet two Welsh-speaking Indians in the dining room of a hotel in Washington, D.C. In considerable detail, they told of their mixed Indian-Welsh heritage and history. They told how the Welsh had come to them after their battles with the Cherokee and had joined with them to create one of the most unique cultural groups in the New World.

preaching the gospel in Welsh. He eventually returned to the British colonies in 1686 where he wrote the story of his adventures.

What became of the Mandan—the tribe into which the Welsh no doubt assimilated? Like so many other Native Americans, they fell victim to an invisible killer, one brought to them by European explorers: smallpox. In 1837 a smallpox epidemic swept through the tribe, almost wiping it out. Today, the Mandan are only four hundred in number, most of whom live on a reservation in North Dakota.

ATLANTIC OCEAN

GREENLAND

ICELAND

NORTH AMERICA

EUROPE

AFRICA

Gulf Stream

Canaries Current

Florida

North Equatorial Current

Mali

Panama

Equatorial Counter Current

South Equatorial Current

SOUTH AMERICA

Peru

N

W   E

S

| 0 | 400 | 800 mi |

| 0 | 400 | 800 km |

CHAPTER 10
GOLDEN SPEARHEADS

Africans
A.D. 1310

Some of the first—and most fascinating—voyages to America before Columbus may have been made centuries ago by black men and women of West Africa.

Many of the crossings were probably accidental. Driven off course by a storm, African fishing and trading vessels would have been at the mercy of powerful currents, and these would have taken them directly to the Americas.

Of those who survived the crossing, many lived in peace with the Native Americans and melded with them through intermarriage. Other Africans established their own separate tribes—and often lived in a constant state of war with the native peoples. Africans sometimes massacred and enslaved Native

This sixth-century wall painting fragment from the Pyramid of Las Higueras, Veracruz, Mexico, shows dark-skinned gods that look more African than Mexican.

Americans, and Native Americans sometimes massacred and enslaved Africans.

Spanish sea captains of the fifteenth century reported seeing black tribes in such places as present-day Florida, Panama, and Peru. Peter Martyr d'Anghera, considered the first historian of America, wrote, "The Spaniards found [blacks] in the province. They only live one day's march from Quarequa [Panama] and they are fierce … and established themselves after the wreck of their ships … the natives of Quarequa carry on incessant war with these [people]."

At least two of the African voyages to the Americas would have had to have been planned.

West African history tells the story of King Abubakari the Second of Mali.

Earlier rulers had extended Mali from the deserts of the north to the jungles of the south. When the young king took the throne in the early 1300s, he had little interest in just continuing to expand the already vast borders of his empire. Abubakari wanted to do something different—something unique and far more exciting. He wanted to see if Earth ended in water, as he had grown up to believe, or if there was other land beyond the horizon.

Under Abubakari's direction, in 1310 a grand fleet was built. It consisted of two hundred wooden ships, all of them more than 100 feet (30 m) long and able to carry up to forty men and women. Each vessel was equipped with both sails and oars, enabling the crew to switch from wind power to manpower as needed. Also, at Abubakari's insistence, a support boat was hitched to every ship, mostly for the purpose of carrying extra food and water.

The day the fleet was to depart, Abubakari called the captains of the ships together. He told them, "Do not return until you have reached the end of the ocean, or when you have exhausted your food and water."

Weeks passed without any news. Then one day, a single ship from the convoy returned to Mali. Summoned to see the king, the captain said, "We sailed for a long while until we came to . . . a strong current flowing in the open sea. My ship was last. The others sailed on. They were pulled out to sea and disappeared."

Upon further questioning, the captain apologized for getting separated and turning back. As to what had become of the others, he had no idea whether they had reached land or still sailed on and on, across an ocean without end.

The word OLMEC *means "rubber people" and comes from the Nahuatl language of the Aztecs.*

After hearing the captain's story, Abubakari decided what he would do. He immediately ordered his craftsmen to build even larger, stronger ships. Two years later, in 1312, he set sail to find out what had become of the first expedition.

The king and his fleet were never seen again.

It is very likely, both expeditions made landfall in present-day Central America, near Panama. The Olmecs, an advanced cultural group of the region, tell the story of black people who had twice come to their land from across the sea in convoys of very large ships.

Were the ships large only in the Olmecs' eyes?

No, not at all.

In 1455 there was an encounter between Portuguese and West African fleets. One of the Portuguese captains wrote, "The [African] vessels slowly approached. . . . They numbered seventeen, and were of considerable size. We estimated that there might be about one hundred and fifty [crew members] on each vessel. The Africans appeared very well built, exceedingly black, and all clothed in [long] white cotton shirts. Some of them wore small white caps on their heads, with a feather in the middle of the cap [to show their rank]. A [soldier] stood in the prow of each boat, with a round shield, probably made of leather. Then they saw two of our vessels advancing towards them. On reaching [their vessels], without any other salute, they threw down their oars and began to shoot off arrows."

In the early 1500s, Spanish explorer Vasco Balboa also saw Africans in Central America. There, Balboa and his crew entered an Indian settlement. To their surprise, they saw a large number of black African war captives. A Spanish historian of the time wrote, "Balboa asked the Indians whence they had [captured them]. They [did not] know more than this, that men of this color were living nearby and they were constantly waging war with them."

Beyond the stories and reports, what other evidence is there of African voyages to the Americas?

In the late nineteenth century, archaeologists began discovering dozens of centuries-old artifacts in Central America and southern Mexico. Among the most baffling were large stone heads sculpted by the Olmecs. Many of the heads had distinctive African features. In addition to being black, the stone faces had full lips, broad noses, and tightly curled hair and beards.

The beards are perhaps the most important feature of all. Olmec men had little or no facial hair and considered it ugly. Any offending hair that sprouted was immediately plucked out.

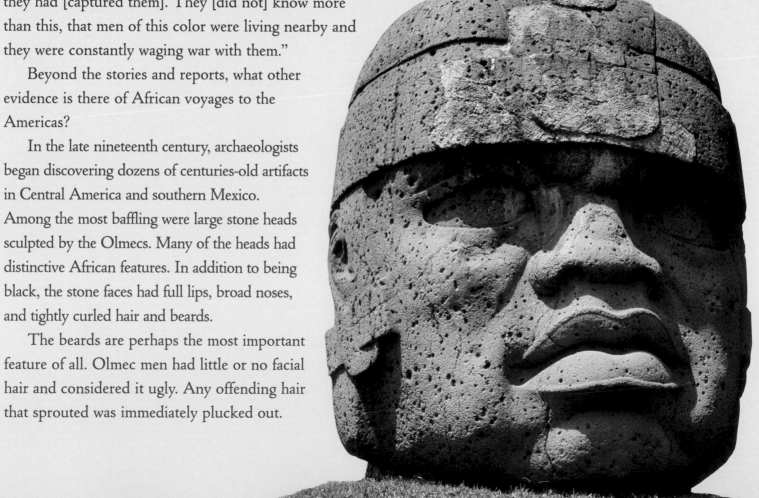

The facial features of this Olmec carving resemble those of African natives.

The Olmecs had perhaps the most unusual spearheads and arrowheads ever known: they were made of gold.

Only one other ethnic group had such weapons: the people of Mali. Spearheads and arrowheads made of gold have been found in several archaeological sites in West Africa. In style and workmanship, those found in Central America and Africa are identical. Moreover, the Olmecs called their golden spearheads *guanin*. In many West African languages, *guanin* means "gold."

It is not known how many Europeans of the fifteenth century had heard of the golden spearheads and African voyages. But one who had was Christopher Columbus. In his diary, he wrote that when he reached present-day Central America, he heard stories of black people who had come from far away. Not only that, but Columbus even collected some of these golden spearheads from the Olmecs and returned home with them. Then he proceeded to have them melted down into gold bars.

In most respects, a West African voyage to America would have been easier than those undertaken 150 years later by Columbus and his crew. For one thing, the distance to the Americas was only half that faced by Columbus. Also, the powerful equatorial current would have further sped the West African vessels to the New World. At most, it would have taken them only thirty days to reach America. Columbus would have been jealous. He and his men were at sea for seventy days—more than two months.

> *Using the most modern techniques, scientists have dated the African stone heads to as early as 800 B.C.*

GREENLAND

ICELAND

Faeroe
Islands

SINCLAIR / ZENO

SINCLAIR / ZENO

NETMAKER'S A.D. 1392

ZENO A.D. 1390

ZENO BROTHERS

EUROPE

Venice

NORTH AMERICA

Nova
Scotia

Westford

BASQUE FISHERMEN

Basque
Region

ATLANTIC OCEAN

AFRICA

N

W   E

S

Caribbean Sea

SOUTH AMERICA

0   315   630 mi

0   315   630 km

Basque Fishermen
Zeno Brothers
Netmaker
Sinclair/Zeno

CHAPTER 11 OTHER PRE-COLUMBIAN VOYAGES

Fourteenth and Fifteenth Centuries

Before Columbus, there were numerous other contacts with the New World. To follow are the stories of just three.

Fish Tale

The Basques are a people living in northern Spain and southwestern France. Though their traditional homeland straddles the border of two nations, they are a close-knit cultural group with their own customs, traditions, and language.

In the eleventh century, Vikings began visiting the region—not to plunder the Basques but to buy dried fish from them. Many Basques were fishers and were expert at curing fish for long voyages such as those the Vikings made across the Atlantic. In fact, Basque fish was a staple of the Vikings' diet when they traveled to America.

From the Vikings, the Basques learned about the great new continent to the west. And they learned how to build ships that were large enough and sturdy enough to travel long distances.

By the fourteenth century, the Basques too were sailing to present-day America—not to explore the land but to fish the seas.

In the waters off the New England coast, they found that whales were plentiful. In small boats launched from their ships, they hunted the mammoth creatures. Just getting close enough to a whale was no easy task. And once one was harpooned, the real excitement—and ugliness—began. Most often the men were taken off on a very long and wild ride. The whale would plow through the seas, dragging the heavy boat behind it, until it became too sick and weak to continue on. Not infrequently, even dying whales turned on the men, and smashed and capsized their boat.

Far less dangerous was hunting cod. The Basques found that North American waters literally teemed with these gray or brown fish usually, around 3 feet (1 m) in length. At the time, the cod were so plentiful they were said to bump into one another when swimming! Often traveling in huge schools just below the surface, they darkened great patches of ocean. A single net could bring in hundreds at a time.

The Basques did not explore the land and made no claim to it. They built no settlements. They only had camps on the beaches during the summer, where they cooked whale blubber into oil and prepared the cod. The codfish were spread open, salted, and then dried in the sun.

In the fall, their ships loaded with barrels of whale oil and dried cod, the men returned to Europe to sell their goods. Among the provisions aboard Columbus's ship were cod and whale oil bought from the Basques.

Sinclair and the Zeno Brothers

Around 1390 a young Venetian nobleman named Nicolo Zeno outfitted a single ship and set sail for the New World. After many days of fair weather and smooth sailing, a fierce storm arose, driving the ship far north of its destination. Its sails in

shreds, huge waves breaking over its decks, it slammed into rocks off the coast of one of the Faeroe Islands in the northern Atlantic. The heaving sea lifted the broken ship off the rocks, and it ground ashore.

Italian explorer Nicolo Zeno was shipwrecked on the Faeroe Islands in about 1390. He was rescued by a group of knights, and many believe Nicolo and his brother Antonio joined the knights in expeditions to America.

The next day, Zeno and his crew found themselves surrounded by fierce Faeroese native peoples intent on murdering them and plundering the ship's cargo. The exhausted and battered sailors were in no condition to defend themselves. They awaited death, resigned to their fate, when, seemingly out of nowhere, a large contingent of knights in armor appeared on the scene. The knights killed many of the Faeroese and scattered the rest.

Nicolo soon learned that Henry Sinclair, a Scottish prince and the ruler of the Faeroes, was in command and had led the rescue. A strong friendship quickly developed between the two. Nicolo wrote to his brother Antonio about his ordeal and salvation by the Scottish prince and suggested that he come to the Faeroes. Antonio arrived within the year.

The Faeroe Islands are located in the North Atlantic, roughly halfway between Norway and Iceland. The inhabitants are mostly of Danish or Scottish ancestry.

Sinclair and brothers Nicolo and Antonio Zeno then proceeded to plan a joint expedition of discovery. They sailed west and landed in Greenland. There, Nicolo became ill and soon died. Antonio, after seeing his brother lowered into his grave, decided to return to Venice. But Sinclair would hear none of it and persuaded him to continue on with the expedition. They again headed west, toward North America, in a fleet of thirteen ships.

The details of the voyage and where the explorers landed are contained in what is known as the Zeno Letters. The letters, found by a descendant of Antonio in an old trunk, were published in book form in the year 1558. At first, readers found the letters fascinating and were convinced that everything in them was true. But as time went on, people began to have doubts. For one thing, the letters contain maps showing islands that no one has been able to find.

But were they really islands? Probably not. Instead, in the opinion of many historians, they were icebergs, which drift and eventually melt and disappear.

People also became skeptical of the letters because they contain descriptions of places that sound too strange to be believed. For example, Antonio wrote of a land in which the ground below them was always on fire and always spewed out smoke. Such a story sounds like a fairy tale.

But is it? In 1950 historian Frederick Pohl went to the province of Nova Scotia, a large peninsula in northeastern Canada. Parts of the region are rich in coal. Many times in recorded history, seams of coal deep underground have caught fire. For months, and even years at a time, the ground underfoot burns, giving off steamy gray smoke.

Thus, Zeno's description is not really far-fetched at all. Instead of showing that he dreamed up a fanciful, nonexistent place, it does the opposite. It shows that he encountered a unique phenomenon that he could only have known about had he been there.

Where did Sinclair and Zeno go next?

From Zeno's letters, it is difficult to tell. His writing is confusing and hard to follow, and it sounds like directions given by a man who himself is lost. In fact, archaeologists would have no clue as to where Sinclair and Zeno wandered in the Northeast if it were not for a large slab of stone unearthed in the 1950s in Westford, Massachusetts. On it is etched a 6-foot (1.8 m) portrait of a knight in armor. The rock is an intriguing find. Still, how do we know that it has any connection with the travels of Zeno and Sinclair? How do we know that they reached Massachusetts?

> The coal in an underground seam can catch on fire as a result of friction created by movement of Earth's crust. In 1832 one huge seam of coal in Nova Scotia burned for almost a year. Only by diverting a river into the seam was the fire finally extinguished.

The knight is holding a shield. And on it is the heraldry, a coat of arms, of the Scottish Gunn clan, cousins of Prince Henry Sinclair. The etched portrait is that of Sir James Gunn, one of the men who accompanied Sinclair to North America, and died there.

Netmaker and the Cannibals

In the Faeroe Islands, a strange and sometimes gruesome tale is told. It is the story of "Netmaker and the Cannibals."

In 1362 four Faeroese fishing vessels, each manned by a crew of twenty or more, headed west to the waters off the American coast. They had almost reached their destination when a powerful storm struck, driving the vessels far apart. What became of three of them is unknown. The fourth, lashed by shrieking winds and mountainous waves, lost its rudder and mainmast—and worse, most of its thirty-two crew members. One after the other, they were swept overboard into the deadly, roiling sea.

When finally the storm passed, the

A Faeroese story says that in the 1390s, a Scottish prince by the name of Henry Sinclair died while exploring America. His companions created a stone carving where he was buried, showing a knight in armor holding a shield with the crest of the clan Gunn. During the late 1800s, a knight was supposedly exhumed at the Westford, Massachusetts, site and taken to the town hall, which subsequently burned. But the stone (above) still *marks the grave.*

survivors, only five in number, drifted in the badly damaged, leaking ship. Without masts or sails, the ship was powerless. Without a rudder, it was directionless.

After many days at sea, the vessel finally ground ashore on an island off Newfoundland, Canada. Native Americans, who referred to their island home as Estotiland, treated the fishers as honored guests. They made sure they were well fed and well taken care of. Those who had been injured were nursed back to health.

One of the most surprising things the crew learned was that other white people had been there before them. "Surely the Vikings had been to Estotiland," wrote one survivor. "They sowed grain and made beer [as the] Northern people do." Too, the Celi Dei had had fairly considerable contact with the native people of Estotiland. In the chief's hut, one of the Scots found what certainly appeared to be evidence of a visit by Christian monks—several books in Latin!

The survivors—especially one of them, a man known as Netmaker—were admired and much sought after for their fishing and other maritime skills. Netmaker had a compass and demonstrated its uses, he showed the people how he could make "ribbed boats" (constructed with overlapping boards), and he was especially skilled at weaving nets. All these things were new to the tribe.

The five men lived contentedly with the Native Americans for ten years. With the chief's blessing, some married women of the tribe.

In 1372 the chief asked Netmaker and his companions to lead an expedition to a group of islands he called Drogio. Its purpose was to attack the native peoples there— cannibals known as Caribs, who coasted the islands and shores of the mainland in search of human prey.

A convoy of twelve small ships headed south. As one of the islands of Drogio came into view, the warriors readied their weapons. But disaster struck even before their attack could begin. In rough seas, all twelve vessels were smashed to pieces on rocks girdling the island. Only Netmaker and a handful of others reached shore.

Struggling from the surf, the survivors, Native American and Faeroese, were immediately captured by the cannibals. And then the real horror began.

The Caribs made elaborate preparations. Then, one by one, the survivors were butchered, cooked, and eaten in a ritualistic and ceremonial manner. As the horrid feast proceeded, Netmaker desperately tried to save himself and his few remaining companions. Frantically, he showed the cannibals how he could make nets, especially with the help of his friends.

The Caribbean Sea is named after the cannibalistic Caribs.

Realizing his captives were of more use to him alive than dead, the headman of the Caribs consented to let them live.

As had happened before on Estotiland, Netmaker came to be held in high regard by the Caribs. News of his special talents—and whereabouts—spread far and wide. When it reached the ears of the Estotilanders, they declared war on the Caribs and recaptured Netmaker.

During the course of the next thirteen years, Netmaker became separated from his companions. He changed hands again and again, going from one Native American tribe to the next. He was kidnapped. He was taken as spoils of war. Most often he was bought and sold, pressed into service as a slave.

Around 1385 Netmaker became a captive of the Maya, who bartered for him in exchange for gold and silver jewelry. For the next three years, he traveled the eastern coast of Mexico, teaching his skills to villagers.

Netmaker was treated well by the Maya, as he had been by other Native Americans. Still, he yearned to return home. Finally, around 1394 he escaped by sea in a small boat of his own making.

Proving that the Atlantic could be crossed by a small vessel, in 1966 John Ridgeway and Chay Blyth rowed across the Atlantic in a boat 20 feet (6 m) long and 8 feet (2.4 m) wide.

Alone, Netmaker sailed from Mexico to his only true friends, the Native Americans of Estotiland. With their help, he built a larger vessel, and after provisioning it, he headed for home—alone. Though Netmaker was an old man by this time, he nevertheless managed to cross the Atlantic. Having survived one of the strangest adventures of all time, he returned to the Faeroes. There, he told his story to anyone who would listen, among them Prince Henry Sinclair and Antonio Zeno.

If Netmaker's story were known only in the Faeroe Islands, it might be dismissed as little more than a wonderful old seaman's yarn. But that's not the case. The same story, from different perspectives, has long been part of the oral histories of the native peoples of Newfoundland, the Caribbean, and Mexico. How could such a tale exist independently in places that are hundreds of miles apart and more than 2,000 miles (3,218 km) from the Faeroes? How, unless, quite simply, it is true?

GREENLAND

ICELAND

NORTH AMERICA

ATLANTIC OCEAN

EUROPE

Portugal

AFRICA

Canary
Islands

A.D. 1492

Guanahani
Island

Cuba

A.D. 1493

A.D. 1502

Panama

Venezuela

A.D. 1498

SOUTH AMERICA

N

W   E

S

0   400   800 mi

0   400   800 km

CHAPTER 12
CHRISTOPHER COLUMBUS

Italian/Spanish
A.D. 1492

As a child, Christopher Columbus was known for his freckled face, red hair, and blue eyes. He had roots in both the Spanish and Italian cultures. Though he was born in the port city of Genoa, Italy, in 1451, his family was Spanish and lived in a Spanish-speaking community. He usually spoke in Spanish and wrote in either that language or Latin, but never Italian.

Because both his father and grandfather were weavers, Christopher learned the trade and spent many hours working a loom or otherwise helping out. But his real interest was the sea. By the age of fourteen, he was studying navigation and sailing small vessels along the southern coast of Europe.

By the age of sixteen, Christopher was working as a crew member on merchant ships. Over the next few years, he traveled to France, Africa, and the Greek island of Chios. He learned to tie sailor's knots, read a compass, handle a tiller, and climb the rigging.

In 1476, when Columbus was twenty-four, the cargo vessel on which he was sailing was attacked and sunk by the French, who were then at war with Italy.

> *Columbus believed the world was shaped like a pear, with Europe at the bottom. Sailing west, he wrote in his papers, caused one "to ascend the stalk to climes that are hotter due to their ever-increasing nearness to the sun."*

Most of the sailors drowned. Clutching an oar and kicking, Columbus managed to swim to the nearest land, Portugal, 6 miles (10 km) away.

Penniless, with only the clothes on his back, Columbus took the first work he could find. He signed aboard a ship that eventually took him to Iceland, a journey frequently made by Europeans of the time. There, he heard stories about the Vikings, Irish, and others who'd traveled to islands and continents to the west. Later, while serving aboard a trading fleet to Africa, he first learned about expeditions launched from Mali many centuries earlier.

The land to the west, Columbus believed, was India. Why? Mostly because of a book, one from his personal library. In it, the famous Greek philosopher Socrates is quoted as saying, "Between the end of Spain and the beginning of India lies a narrow sea that can be sailed in a few days."

Columbus tried to interest the king and queen of Spain—Ferdinand and Isabella—in financing a voyage. It took eight very long, difficult years, but he finally succeeded. On August 3, 1492, the *Niña*, the *Pinta*, and the *Santa Maria* sailed down the Tinto River and out into the Atlantic. For Columbus, aboard the *Santa Maria*, it was his first command of a ship, not to mention a fleet.

Seventy days later, at two o'clock in the morning of

Christopher Columbus (left) *worked for many years to convince King Ferdinand* (right) *and Queen Isabella* (center) *of Spain to finance his voyage to the New World.*

Eighteen of the ninety crew members on Columbus's first voyage to the Americas were teenagers.

Columbus enslaved seven native people of Guanahani, took them back to Spain with him, and used them as evidence of his discovery of the New World.

October 12, 1492, a sailor named Rodrigo de Triana spotted the dark outline of land. Columbus, roused from his sleep, quickly made his way above deck. It must have been an incredible moment for him. He believed he had, at long last, reached India by sailing west.

At sunrise, with the captains of the other two ships, he went ashore on the Caribbean island of Guanahani (now San Salvador). There, he planted the royal banner of Spain. And for the next four hundred years, he was known as the discoverer of America.

Why, when so many others had been to the New World before him?

The names of Columbus's three ships, the Niña, Pinta, *and* Santa Maria, *are well known to every schoolchild who learns of Columbus's trip to America.*

One reason was the printing press. Invented fifty-two years before Columbus's first voyage, news of the explorer's success quickly spread far and wide. Books and pamphlets were written about him. Most correctly praised him as a skilled navigator and brave adventurer but also incorrectly named him as the first nonnative to reach the new land by sea.

Columbus returned to Europe to a hero's welcome. Summoned by the king and queen of Spain, he and his crew—and captive Caribbean slaves—paraded through town after town on their way to the royal reception. People lined the streets and waved from balconies, cheering them on.

The fact that royalty financed the expedition also caused Columbus's voyage to receive a great deal of special attention. Ferdinand and Isabella, as king and queen of Spain, made sure that monarchs in all other European countries were aware that they had found the land and claimed it as their own.

Very important, too, was the fact that Columbus did not make just one voyage to America—he made four. Not only were they well publicized, but they were proof that the Atlantic could be crossed repeatedly. Inspired by Columbus's example, numerous other European explorers—especially

Columbus came ashore in the West Indies and Central and South America, but he never actually set foot in North America.

* * * *

During his second voyage to America in 1493, Columbus had several of his men hanged for disobedience.

* * * *

In 1472, twenty years before Columbus's voyage to the Americas, a Portuguese sailor named Jao Corte-Real sailed to America. However, because the expedition's goal—finding a sea route to Asia—was not achieved, Corte-Real's voyage was dismissed as a failure. It was considered an embarrassment and rarely spoken of—until the real potential of the New World became obvious. The Corte-Real voyage was then proclaimed as evidence of Portuguese rights to part of the New World—a proclamation that gained little attention.

During Columbus's four Atlantic crossings and returns, he lost nine ships. The first of those to sink was the Santa Maria. *It went down during a storm in the Caribbean shortly after midnight on Christmas Eve, 1492.*

* * * *

In May 1998, Warren White and his son were swimming off the coast of Panama when they spotted an ancient wreck sporting two huge, barnacle-encrusted cannons. The wreck is believed to be the Viscaina, *one of Columbus's ships, which sank in 1503 during his last voyage across the Atlantic.*

Dutch, French, Spanish, and English—soon launched their own expeditions.

Following in the wake of the explorers, settlers came in ever-increasing numbers. Most were the poor and oppressed of Europe. They knew very little about the new land, only that it was wild, dangerous, and rich with opportunity. As to its history, they knew almost nothing, only that Christopher Columbus had discovered it.

Though Columbus was certainly not the first to reach America by sea, he nevertheless had the strongest impact on its history. His discovery launched a massive migration of Europeans to the American continents and set into motion the creation of the Americas as they exist today.

Source Notes

12 Charles M. Boland, *They All Discovered America* (Garden City, NY: Doubleday 1961), 38.

14 Ibid., 32.

24 Ibid., 54.

26 Ibid., 61.

30 Fang Zhongpu, "Chinese Buddhists Reach America 1,000 Years Before Columbus?" *China Reconstructs.* 29, no. 8 (August 1980): 65.

31 Linda Matthews, "Chinese Claim Another First," *Los Angeles Times*, July 13, 1981, 1.

32–33 Zhongpu, 65.

33 Ibid, 65.

39 Gavin Menzies, *1492—The Year China Discovered America* (New York: HarperCollins, 2004), 463.

46 Boland, 119.

51 Ibid., 133.

51 Ibid., 122.

55 Paul Halsall, "Modern History Sourcebook: The Discovery of North America by Leif Ericsson, c. 1000—from the Saga of Eric the Red, 1387," *Modern History Sourcebook*, 1998, http://www.fordham.edu/halsall/mod/1000Vinland.html (February 28, 2007).

55–56 Boland, 162.

56 Ibid.

56 Ibid., 163.

62 Halsall, "Modern History," 2.

63 Boland, 177.

64 Halsall, "Modern History," 3.

68 Wisconsin State Historical Society, "The Vinland History of the Flat Island Book," *American Journeys*, 2003, http://content.wisconsinhistory.org/cdm4/document.php?CISOROOT=/aj&CISOPTR=4209&CISOSHOW=3295&REC=16 (February 28,2007).

68 Ibid, 53.

68 Ibid.

69 Paul Halsall, "Thorvald Goes to Wineland," *Modern History Sourcebook*, 1998, http://www.fordham.edu/halsall/mod/1000Vinland/html (February 28, 2007).

69 Ibid.

69 Ibid.

69 Ibid.

74 Boland, 203.

74 "The Saga of Thorfinn Karlsefni," *Internet Sacred Text Archive*, n.d., http://www.sacred-texts.com/neu/nda/nda20.htm (February 28, 2007).

74 Boland, 223.

75 Ibid.

75 Paul Halsall, "Freydis Causes the Brothers to Be Put to Death," *Modern History Sourcebook*, 1998, http://www.fordham.edu/halsall/mod/1000Vinland.html. (February 28, 2007).

76 Boland, 223–224.

85 Richard Deacon, *Madoc and the Discovery of America* (London: Frederick Muller, 1966), 9.

88 Howard Kimberley, *Madoc, Madoc 1170*, December 2006, http://www.madoc1170.com/evidence.htm (May 11, 2007).

92 Ivan Van Sertima, *They Came before Columbus: African Presence in Ancient America* (New York: Random House, 1976), 21–22.

92 Jim Haskins, *Against All Opposition: Black Explorers in America* (New York: Walker and Co., 1992), 2.

93 Van Sertima, 46–47.

93–94 Ibid., 51–52.

94 Ibid., 21.

103 Boland, 329.

108 Zachary Kent, *The World's Greatest Explorers: Columbus* (Chicago: Children's Press, 1989), 18.

SELECTED BIBLIOGRAPHY

BOOKS

Barden, Renardo. *The Discovery of America.* San Diego: Greenhaven Press, 1989.

Barrow, R. H. *The Romans.* Baltimore: Penguin Books, 1949.

Baudez, Claude. *Lost Cities of the Mayas.* New York: Harry N. Abrams, 1992.

Begley, Sharon. "The First Americans." *Newsweek,* Fall–Winter 1991, 15–20.

Bender, David, and Bruno Leon, eds. *Christopher Columbus and His Legacy: Opposing Viewpoints.* San Diego: Greenhaven Press, 1992.

Boak, Arthur. *A History of Rome to 565 AD.* New York: Macmillan, 1943.

Boland, Charles. *They All Discovered America.* Garden City, NY: Doubleday, 1961.

Borstin, Daniel. *The Americans: The Colonial Experience.* New York: Random House, 1958.

Chidester, David. *Christianity.* New York: HarperCollins, 2000.

Claiborne, Robert, ed. *The First Americans.* New York: Time-Life Books, 1974.

Collins, Michael. *The Story of Christianity.* New York: DK Publishing, 1999.

Collis, John. *Christopher Columbus.* New York: Stein and Day, 1976.

Deacon, Richard. *Madoc and the Discovery of America.* London: Frederick Muller, 1966.

Donnelly, Ivon. *Chinese Junks.* London: Keely and Walsh, 1920.

Faber, Harold. *The Discoverers of America.* New York: Charles Scribner's Sons, 1992.

Fell, Barry. *America BC.* New York: Times Book Company, 1976.

Fiske, John. *The Discovery of America.* 2 vols. New York: Houghton Mifflin, 1892.

Foster, Lynn V. *A Brief History of Mexico.* New York: Facts on File, 1997.

Fowler, William. "The Westford Indian Rock." *Bulletin of the Massachusetts Archaeological Society,* 1960.

Friedman, Robert, ed. *The Life Millennium, The 100 Most Important Events and People of the Past 1,000 Years.* New York: Time-Life Books, 1998.

Godfrey, William S. "The Newport Tower II," *Archaeology,* Summer 1950, 17–21.

Goodwin, William B. *The Ruins of Great Ireland in New England.* Boston: Meador, 1946.

Grant, Michael. *The World of Rome.* Cleveland: World, 1975.

Griffin, M. T. *Nero: The End of a Dynasty.* London: Batsford; New Haven, CT: Yale, 1985.

Harden, Donald. *The Phoenicians.* London: Thames and Hudson, 1962.

Hogvgaard, William. "The Norsemen in Greenland," *Geological Review,* 15, no. 4 (October 1925): 20–26.

Jackson, Donald. *Who the Heck Did Discover the New World?* Washington, DC: Smithsonian Institution Press, 1991.

James, Simon. *Ancient Rome.* London: Dorling Kindersley Books, 1990.

Katz, Solomon. "The Roman Legacy." In Mortimer Chambers, ed. *The Fall of Rome: Can It Be Explained?* New York: Holt, Rinehart, and Winston, 1963.

Kurlansky, Mark. *The Cod's Tale.* New York: G. P. Putnam's Sons, 2001.

Lane, Fox. *Pagans and Christians.* San Francisco: Penguin, 1988.

Lemonic, Michael D., and Andrea Dorfman. "The Amazing Vikings." *Time,* May 8, 2000, 68–74.

Mathews, Linda. "Chinese Claim Another First." *Los Angeles Times,* July 13, 1981.

Menzies, Gavin. *1421—The Year China Discovered America.* New York: HarperCollins, 2003.

Miller, Robert. *Mexico—A History.* Norman: University of Oklahoma Press, 1974.

Moscati, Sabatino. *The World of the Phoenicians.* London: Orion Publishing Group, 1965.

Nardo, Don. *From Founding to Fall: A History of Rome.* Farmington Mills, MI: Lucent Books, 2003.

————. *The Rise of Christianity.* San Diego: Greenhaven Press, 1999.

Odijk, Pamela. *The Phoenicians.* Englewood Cliffs, NJ: Silver Burdett Press, 1989.

————. *The Vikings.* Englewood Cliffs, NJ: Silver Burdett Press, 1989.

Peterson, Mendel L. *History under the Sea.* Washington, DC: Smithsonian Institution Publication 4,174, 1954.

Pohl, Frederick J. *Atlantic Crossings Before Columbus.* New York: W. W. Norton, 1961.

————. *The Lost Discovery—Uncovering the Track of the Vikings in America.* New York: W. W. Norton, 1952.

————. *The Viking Settlements of North America.* New York: Clarkson N. Potter, 1972.

Qianzhi, Zhu. *The First Collection of Biographies of Famous Monks.* Vol. 9. Groningen, NL: Kemper, 1937.

————. *Textual Research on Fusang.* Groningen, NL: Kemper, 1941.

Scarre Chris. *Chronicle of the Romans.* London: Thames and Hudson, 1995.

Schwartz, Robert. *The Roman Empire.* Lanham, MD: University Press of America, 1998.

Scullard, H. H. *From the Gracchi to Nero. A History of Rome 133 BC to AD 68.* 5th ed. New York: Routledge Press, 1982.

Sertima, Ivan Van. *They Came Before Columbus: African Presence in Ancient America*. New York: Random House, 1976.

Sharer, Robert J. *The Ancient Maya*. 5th ed. Stanford, CA: Stanford University Press, 1994.

Sharp, Andrew. *Ancient Voyages in the Pacific*. Baltimore: Pelican, 1957.

Sjovold, Thorlief. *The Oseberg Find*. Oslo: Universitietes Oldsaksamling, 1957.

Smart, T. H. *The Flatey Book and Recently Discovered Vatican Manuscripts Concerning America as Early as the Tenth Century*. New York: Norroena Society, 1906.

Smith, Marion, ed. *Asia and North America: Transpacific Contacts*. Salt Lake City: Society for American Archaeology, 1953.

Sordi, M. *The Christians and the Roman Empire*. Norman: University of Oklahoma Press, 1988.

Stein, Conrad. *The Pilgrims*. Chicago: Children's Press, 1995.

Stuart, George E. *The Mysterious Maya*. New York: National Geographic Society, 1977.

Suetonius. *Lives of the Twelve Caesars*. Translated by Joseph Gavorse. New York: Modern Library, 1931.

Tacitus, P./Corneluis, *The Annals*. In *Great Books of the Western World*. Vol. 15., translated by Alfred Church. Chicago: Encyclopaedia Britannica, 1952.

Thalbitzer, William. *Two Runic Stones from Greenland and Minnesota*. Washington, DC: Smithsonian Institution, 1951.

Trout, Lawana Hooper. *The Maya*. New York: Chelsea House, 1991.

Visalli, Gayla, ed. *After Jesus*. Pleasantville, NY: Reader's Digest, 1992.

Warmington, B. H. *Suetonius: Nero*. Bristol, UK: Bristol Classical Press, 1981.

Willoughby, Charles C. *Antiquities of the New England Indians.* Cambridge, MA: Harvard University Press, 1935.

Yue, Charlotte, and David Yue. *Christopher Columbus.* Boston: Houghton Mifflin, 1992.

Zhongpu, Fang. "Chinese Buddhists Reach America 1,000 Years Before Columbus?" *China Reconstructs.* Vol. 29, (August 1980): 65–66.

WEBSITES

AFRICAN

Hagen, W. Robert. "Laying the Foundations: Pre-Columbian Exploration and Colonization of the New World." *Millersville University.* N.d.
http://muweb.millersville.edu/~columbus/papers/wrhagen.html (November 7, 2006).

Oxford University Press, "Africa and the Discovery of America." Oxford Journals, *African Affairs.* N.d.
http://afraf.oxfordjournals.org/cgi/content/citation/XXIII/XC/163 (November 7, 2006).

CHINESE

BBC News. "Experts hope to emulate Chinese Columbus." *BBC World News. Science and Nature.* October 22, 2002.
http://news.bbc.co.uk/2/hi/science/nature/2349929.stm, (November 6, 2006).

Gidney, Charlie. "Map Bolsters America-Discovery Claim." *China Daily,* January 17, 2006.
http://www.chinadaily.com.cn/english/doc/2006-01/17/content_512772.htm (November 6, 2006).

Leland, Charles G. "Fusang." *Sacred Texts.* N.d.
http://www.sacred-texts.com/earth/fu/index.htm (November 6, 2006).

Menzies, Gavin. *1421, The Year China Discovered the World.* N.d.
http://www.1421.tv/ (November 6, 2006).

People's Daily. "Chinese Explorer Credited With Discovery of America." March 7, 2002. Available online at *China.org.cn.* N.d.
http://www.china.org.cn/english/2002/Mar/28263.htm (November 6, 2006).

Pine Street Foundation. "Discover." *Pine Street Foundation.* N.d.,
http://www.psmerg.org/chinalanding/articles/DISCOVER.htm (November 6, 2006).

COLUMBUS

Center for the Public Domain and the University of North Carolina at Chapel Hill. "Christopher Columbus." *ibiblio.* N.d.
http://www.ibiblio.org/expo/1492.exhibit//c-Columbus/columbus.html (November 7, 2006).

Cortez, Vanessa. "The Startling Myths—And Facts!—About Christopher Columbus." *Weekly Universe,* October 8, 2001.
http://www.weeklyuniverse.com/columbus.htm (November 7, 2006).

Kagan, Richard L. ""The Discovery of Columbus." *Millersville University.* October 6, 1991.
http://muweb.millersville.edu/~columbus/data/rev/KAGAN-01.REV (November 7. 2006).

IRISH

Newfoundland and Labrador Heritage. "Exploration and Settlement." *Newfoundland and Labrador Heritage.* N.d.
http://www.heritage.nf.ca/exploration/ (November 6, 2006).

Northvegr Foundation. "Chapter IV. Discovery Of America By The Irish." *Northvegr Foundation.* N.d.
http://www.northvegr.org/lore/norse/044.php (November 6, 2006).

———. "Chapter III. Columbus And The Norsemen." *Northvegr Foundation.* N.d., http://www.northvegr.org/lore/norse/043.php (November 6, 2006).

Reeves, Arthur Middleton, North Ludlow Beamish, and Rasmus B. Anderson. "The Norse Discovery of America." *Sacred Texts.* N.d. http://www.sacred-texts.com/neu/nda/index.htm (November 6, 2006).

Washburn, Wilcomb. "Exploration and Discovery before 1492, from the Chistopher Columbus Encyclopedia, Vol. 1, 1992." *Millersville University.* N.d. http://muweb.millersville.edu/~columbus/data/art/WASHBR12.ART (November 6, 2006).

OTHER PRE-COLUMBIAN VOYAGES

New Advent. "Hernando Cortés." *Catholic Encyclopeida.* N.d. http://www.newadvent.org/cathen/04397a.htm (November 7, 2006).

Reeves, Arthur Middleton, North Ludlow Beamish, and Rasmus B. Anderson. "Voyage of Gudleif Gudlaugson to Great Ireland." *Sacred Texts.* N.d. http://www.sacred-texts.com/neu/nda/nda25.htm (November 6, 2006).

Wikipedia Encyclopedia. "Age of Discovery." *Wikipedia.* November 7, 2006. http://en.wikipedia.org/wiki/Age_of_Discovery (November 7, 2006).

PHOENICIAN

Dankenbring, William F. "Who Really Discovered America?" *Hope of Israel Ministries.* N.d. http://hope-of-israel.org/hebinusa.htm (November 7, 2006).

Phoenician Canaanite Encyclopedia. "Did the Phoenicians Discover the New World?" *Phoenica.org.* N.d. http://phoenicia.org/america.html (November 7, 2006).

ROMAN

Stewart, Rixon. "America Before Columbus." *The Truth Seeker.* January 9, 2006.
http://www.thetruthseeker.co.uk/article.asp?ID=139 (November 7, 2006).

VIKING

Alden, Jan. "Sagas on the Trail to Vinland." Americas 48, January–February 1996: 6–13.

Fordham University. "The Discovery of North America by Leif Ericsson c. 1000 from the Saga of Eric the Red, 1387." *Modern History Sourcebook.* July 22, 2006.
http://www.fordam.edu/halsall/mod/1000Vinland.html (October 31, 2006).

Gerrard, Nelson S. "The Land They Left." The Emigration of Iceland to North America. October 12, 2003.
http://www.halfdan.is/vestur/why.htm (November 6, 2006).

Ryne, Linn. "Leif Ericson, Columbus' Predecessor by Nearly 500 Years." ODIN. N.d.
http://www.mnc.net/norway/ericson.htm (November 6, 2006).

WELSH

Clarke, G. "Prince Madoc Discovers America." *Valley Stream.* N.d.
http://www.valleystream.co.uk/madoc.htm (November 6, 2006).

Historic UK. "The Discovery of America . . . by a Welsh Prince?" *Historic UK.com.* N.d.
http://www.historic-uk.com/HistoryUK/Wales-History/DiscoveryofAmerica.htm (November 6, 2006).

Kimberley, Howard. "Were the Welsh the First European Americans?" *Madoc 1170.* March 2000.
http://www.madoc1170.com/home.htm (November 6, 2006).

Wanner, Jayne. "A Consideration: Was America Discovered In 1170 by Prince Madoc Ab Owain Gwynedd Of Wales?" N.d. http://www.tylwythteg.com/fortmount/Ftmount.html (May 15, 2007).

Wikimedia Foundation. "Madoc." *Wikipedia*. October 31, 2006. http://en.wikipedia.org/wiki/Madog (November 6, 2006).

Young, Simon. "Voyage Beyond the Sea." *Fortean Times*. October 2001. http://www.forteantimes.com/articles/151_stbrendan.shtml (November 6, 2006).

Further Reading and Websites

BOOKS

Cotterell, Arthur. *Ancient China.* New York: DK Books, 1994.

Day, Nancy. *Your Travel Guide to the Ancient Mayan Civilization.* Minneapolis: Twenty-First Century Books, 2001.

Goldstein, Margaret J. *Lebanon in Pictures.* Minneapolis: Twenty-First Century Books, 2005.

Greene, Carol. *Christopher Columbus: A Great Explorer.* Chicago: Children's Press, 1989.

Haskins, Jim. *Against All Opposition: Black Explorers in America.* New York: Walker, 1992.

Humble, Richard. *The Age of Leif Eriksson.* London: Franklin Watts, 1989.

Kent, Zachary. *The World's Great Explorers.* Chicago: Children's Press, 1989.

Kerrigan, Michael. *Ancient Rome and the Roman Empire.* New York: DK Publishing, 2001.

Markel, Rita J. *Your Travel Guide to Ancient Rome.* Minneapolis: Twenty-First Century Books, 2004.

Nardo, Don. *The Roman Empire.* San Diego: Lucent Books, 1994.

Pelta, Kathy. *Discovering Christopher Columbus.* Minneapolis: Twenty-First Century Books, 1991.

Sertima, Ivan Van. *They Came Before Columbus: African Presence in Ancient America.* New York: Random House, 1976.

Sherman, Josepha. *Your Travel Guide to Ancient China.* Minneapolis: Twenty-First Century Books, 2004.

Sordi, M. *The Christians and the Roman Empire.* Norman: University of Oklahoma Press, 1988.

Stefoff, Rebecca. *The Viking Explorers.* New York: Chelsea House, 1993.

Woods, Michael, and Mary B. Woods. *Ancient Transportation.* Minneapolis: Twenty-First Century Books, 2000.

WEBSITES

African Sailors and a Vanished Colony
  http://www.texancultures.utsa.edu/publications/exploration/chapternine.htm
  This site has detailed discussions of the evidence of African voyages and settlements in America, ca. 1311.

Discovery of Greenland in America
  http://www.iceland.is/history-and-culture/History/Discovery-of-America/
  An accounting of the life of Erik the Red and his son Leif as translated from the Icelandic sagas can be found on this website. It also features the Saga of Erik the Red and the Saga of the Greenlanders.

The Discovery of North America by Leif Ericsson, c. 1000 from the Saga of Eric the Red, 1387
  http://www.fordham.edu/halsall/mod/1000Vinland.html
  This website includes an account of Leif Ericsson's journey to North America as translated from the *Flateyiarbok* compiled by Jon Thordharson in about 1387.

Laying the Foundation: Pre-Columbian Exploration and Colonization of the New World
  http://homepages.rootsweb.com/~lrnoah/NCOrange/early.htm
  Accounting and discussion of various pre-Columbian contacts with America, including those by Phoenicians, West Africans, and Irish, can be found on this website.

Thorvald Ericsson
  http://famousamericans.net/thorvaldericsson
  The story of Thorvald Ericsson's explorations in North America, his encounters with Native Americans, and his death are featured on this website.

Thorvald's Rock
  http://www.viking.no/e/info-sheets/usa/thorvald.htm
  This site has description and discussion of Thorvald Ericsson's burial site in New Hampshire.

INDEX

About the Author

Don Wulffson is the author of more than forty books, including *Point Blank, Toys, The Upside-Down Ship, Aliens, Future Fright,* and *The Kid Who Invented the Popsicle*. His young adult novel *Soldier X* received a Christopher medal and other awards.

Wulffson is also the author of numerous educational programs and more than three hundred stories, poems, and nonfiction pieces. He has been selected four times as an Outstanding Educator in America and is the recipient of the Distinguished Achievement Award for his educational writing and the Leather Medal Award for his poetry.

Photo Acknowledgments

The images in this book are used with permission of: PhotoDisc Royalty Free by Getty Images, all backgrounds; © Danny Lehman/CORBIS, p. 5; Jeff Del Nero, pp. 6, 16, 28, 40, 52, 58, 66, 78, 82, 90, 96, 106; © North Wind Picture Archives, pp. 7, 21, 69, 75, 81, 108, 109; © Roger Viollet/Getty Images, p. 8; Dawn Roberson/America's Stonehenge, pp. 10, 11; © Danielle Carnito/Independent Picture Service, pp. 12, 27; Library of Congress, p. 19 (ppmsc 03509); © SSPL/The Image Works, p. 23; © Snark/Art Resource, NY, p. 31; Drawing by Linda Schele, © David Schele, courtesy Foundation for the Advancement of the Mesoamerican Studies, Inc., www.famsi.org, p. 32; © Hong Nian Zhang/National Geographic Image Collection, p. 33; The Art Archive/National Anthropological Museum Mexico/Dagli Orti, p. 34 (top); The Art Archive/Genius of China Exhibition, p. 34 (bottom); © Frederic J. Brown/AFP/Getty Images, p. 36; © Jax Museum of Modern Art/SuperStock, p. 38; © fstop2/Alamy, p. 43; © Mary Evans Picture Library/Alamy, pp. 45, 84; © Werner Forman/CORBIS, pp. 49, 61; © Tom Bean/CORBIS, p. 50; © Hulton Archive/Getty Images, p. 53; The Mariners' Museum, Newport News, VA, p. 54; © Bettmann/CORBIS, p. 59; © Bridgeman Art Library, London/SuperStock, p. 63; © Wolfgang Kaehler/CORBIS, p. 64; The Hampton Historical Society, p. 70; University Museum of Cultural Heritage, Oslo, Norway, p. 73; © Visual Arts Library (London)/Alamy, p. 79; © AA World Travel Library/Alamy, p. 83; © Smithsonian American Art Museum, Washington, DC/Art Resource, NY, p. 87; The Art Archive/Xalapa Museum Veracruz Mexico/Dagli Orti, p. 91; © Werner Forman/Art Resource, NY, p. 94; © Mary Evans Picture Library, p. 99; Joanna Rathe- Boston Globe, p. 102. Front cover: © Knudsens-Giraudon/Art Resource, NY. Back cover: Jeff Del Nero.